Endangered Guardians

Endangered Guardians

*Party Reform within a
Constitutional System*

Donald V. Weatherman

ROWMAN & LITTLEFIELD PUBLISHERS, INC.

ROWMAN & LITTLEFIELD PUBLISHERS, INC.

Published in the United States of America
by Rowman & Littlefield Publishers, Inc.
4720 Boston Way, Lanham, Maryland 20706

3 Henrietta Street
London WC2E 8LU, England

British Cataloging in Publication Information Available

Library of Congress Cataloging-in-Publication Data

Weatherman, Donald V., 1947–
  Endangered guardians : party reform within a constitutional system
/ Donald V. Weatherman.
     p. cm.
Includes bibliographical references and index.
1. Political parties—United States—History. 2. United States—
Constitutional history. I. Title.
JK2261.W43 1994 324.273'009—dc20 94-3809 CIP

ISBN 0–8476–7965–9 (cloth: alk. paper)
ISBN 0–8476–7966–7 (pbk: alk. paper)

Printed in the United States of America

 ™ The paper used in this publication meets the minimum requirements of
American National Standard for Information Sciences—Permanence of
Paper for Printed Library Materials, ANSI Z39.48–1984.

To my Parents

Contents

Preface

This volume is the result of three driving passions. The first is a passion to understand the true origins of the American party system. The second is a passion to defend the Founders' great insight into the necessary workings of a republican government. The third has to do with my passion as an educator, to explain to those who are skeptical such matters that seem obvious to me. Over the past two decades I have encountered a number of delightfully skeptical students; they serve in my classroom a function similar to what my first cup of coffee does for my day. I hope this work will stimulate further investigation into the true origins and development of our party system, for no scholar has yet adequately described how political parties began in America nor the significant implication of what their origins mean to their continued mission within our overall political system.

The importance of a clear understanding of the true origins and purpose of the American party system was underlined for me in 1988 when I was preparing testimony for the Rules and Administration Committee of the U.S. Senate. The Senate was discussing a regional primaries bill, and I was asked to describe why such a bill might not be in the best interest of the nation. One of my main arguments was that the nominating process should test candidates' ability to excel in the general election that follows the nomination process. Maintaining a parallel process in the two types of elections was of considerable importance. As my research continued, it was clear that the nomination process was little more than a means to the end of winning the general election; it became equally clear that the general election itself was no more than a means to yet another end. In the final analysis, all this political manuevering should be driven by a desire for what ought to be the ultimate end of all political activity—good government.

If the above argument is valid, then everything we do in our political system must be guided by our definition of good government. Unfortunately, discussions about such matters seem beyond the reach of the usual debates on policy matters in the Senate and elsewhere. A year later when I was asked to submit testimony to the same committee on campaign finance legislation, I was confronted by the same dilemma. This time the stakes seemed even higher. Legislators can discuss matters affecting the executive branch with greater detachment than they can matters directly affecting themselves. This second debate on campaign finance reform reminded me of Publius's assertion that no individual or group should judge in matters that affect them directly.

In both of these discussions there appeared to be little appreciation and even less understanding of the delicate yet vital role political parties play in our overall political system. The concerns expressed by politicians and pundits alike were far more focused on their perceptions of short-term partisan or institutional advantage than on the effects these reforms would have on the overall workings of our complex political system.

This short volume is a result of my dissatisfaction with the available literature on the proper relationship between the American two-party system and the Constitution. By focusing on reform efforts, I have attempted to examine those periods when this relationship should have been discussed in its fullest detail. What I have found was that these discussions either did not attempt to reconcile the party system with the constitutional system or, when they did, revealed very little sympathy toward our constitutional system.

I approached this topic with reservations. The first was that there are several widely published authors who might bring to the topic a more extensive knowledge of the literature in this field; the second has to do with my teacher, Harry V. Jaffa. When I was in graduate school some twenty years ago, he would often discuss the books he read in the evenings before going to bed. My image at that time was that his daytime reading was devoted to such authors as Abraham Lincoln, Winston Churchill, Aristotle, or his teacher, Leo Strauss. His evenings were reserved for reading less demanding and usually secondary works. I hope this volume will be deemed worthy for his bedside table.

My debt to Professor Jaffa is truly great. I often tell my students that he saved me from law school, and the legal profession from me. He was also instrumental in guiding me into an academic career instead of a political one. Words can hardly describe how grateful I am on both counts. Yet both of these contributions to my life pale in comparison to a third contribution he made. He and Mrs. Jaffa played a significant role in my coming to know Lynn Blyth, to whom I have been happily married for over twenty years now.

Lynn has been my main literary critic and a superb editor during these past two decades. She is the only person who read this manuscript before it was sent to the publisher. What a friend she is. Others have been helpful in this endeavor as well. Gretchen Logan meticulously edited the endnotes and never overlooked details. The people at Rowman & Littlefield have been very helpful, as well: Jonathan Sisk, the anonymous reviewers, and, especially, freelance editor Lynn Gemmell. Dean Covington and his able staff at the Lyon College library have been more than generous with their time and expertise.

The family of John Dyer Trimble Sr. generously provided the funds for the professorship I currently hold. They epitomize the attributes I associate with gracious Southern families.

Two other important people in my life are David and Andrea. Their patience with me during this project has not always been duly acknowledged but is truly appreciated. They are wonderful children who help me maintain my perspective.

Donald V. Weatherman
Batesville, Arkansas

Acknowledgments

I have received generous support for the research and writing of this book. The Lynde and Harry Bradley Foundation supported the early stages of my research while I was a Bradley Scholar at the Heritage Foundation. The Earhart Foundation supported the research and writing of the chapter on Woodrow Wilson. This was the second time they extended me research support and I am indeed grateful for their confidence in my work. This project was completed while I was on sabbatical leave from Arkansas College (now Lyon College).

Introduction

Endangered Guardians

> Both our political parties, at least the honest part of them, agree
> conscientiously in the same object—the public good; but they
> differ essentially in what they deem the means of promoting that
> good. One side believes it best done by one composition of the
> governing powers; the other, by a different one. One fears most
> the ignorance of the people; the other, the selfishness of rulers
> independent of them.
> —Thomas Jefferson

Political parties have always posed a special problem to students of American politics. For some students, the problem is a result of parties' extra-constitutional nature; for others it is the general role and purpose of political parties within our overall political system. For most, the problem parties present is a result of their strange origin and development within the American regime. But we must remember that the unintended development and extraconstitutional nature of parties hardly make them unique. The U.S. Constitution, as is well documented, was intended as a skeleton for our government; in time, certain precedents would develop, out of necessity or convenience, that would complement our basic constitutional structure. Our enlightened founders left enough flexibility in our system to permit growth and maturation. A close reading of the notes kept during the Constitutional Convention of 1787 makes it obvious that some issues were intentionally left to be decided by time and circumstances.

For this reason, the first Congress of the United States is often referred to as a second Constitutional Convention. It was the first Congress that proposed the Bill of Rights, created the first cabinet positions, and developed the basic structure of our federal court system. After these accomplishments, a national party division started to emerge. Joseph Charles described the first glimpse of party division:

1

The group that had traveled so far together as a reasonably compact band came to the main fork in the road, not with the framing and adoption of the Constitution, but during the 1790's. How to administer machinery newly set up, what concrete meaning, in unforeseen contingencies, to give to words which no longer meant the same thing to all: these were the new problems which weakened old ties and sharpened earlier differences.[1]

Thomas Jefferson emerged as the symbolic leader of the developing opposition but James Madison was its chief architect.

Clarification of Madison's role in the development of our national party system can increase our understanding of the fundamental compatibility between our constitutional and party systems. Madison's role in the development of party politics in America is greatly misunderstood. Authors like James MacGregor Burns who credit Jefferson with founding the Republican party skip Madison's crucial contribution to party development. Others seem determined to use Madison's argument in *Federalist* 10 to discredit anything he said or did after the Constitution was ratified.

Two of the most influential and oft-quoted works on the origins of America's party system are Joseph Charles's *The Origins of the American Party System* and Richard Hofstadter's *The Idea of a Party System*. These are both fine historical works that chronicle some of the most important events surrounding America's party development, but both authors underestimated the importance the constitutional system played in the early stage of party development. Charles focused primarily on the events that surrounded the early party development, and Hofstadter seemed committed to perpetuating the notion of "Jeffersonian democracy."

But each of these works has captured an important component of our party development. Charles acknowledged the central role Madison performed in the first stage of our party development and Hofstadter recognized the important role Martin Van Buren performed in the second stage of our party development.

Jefferson was indeed an influential and thoughtful personality during the founding period but the role he played in shaping early American party politics was largely symbolic. John Chester Miller concisely and accurately sketched the roles Jefferson and Madison performed in our young republic when he argued:

Upon every score except that of service to the cause of American Independence, Madison's stature was equal to that of Jefferson, and in one particular—the work of organizing the Republican party and equipping it with a political philosophy—his contribution was even greater than that of his fellow Virginian.[2]

Charles echoed this belief when he referred to Jefferson as a "late recruit to an opposition already led by James Madison." Charles further revealed that "it was Madison who was regarded by the Federalists as their principal adversary."[3] Miller understood the importance of Madison's role in party development, in part, because he realized that "political parties first manifested themselves in Congress" and then later "percolated down to the electorate."[4] There is considerable disagreement over how and when the percolating took place, but recognizing that America's parties began as congressional parties is of great importance. One of the reasons many people have been unable to appreciate fully Madison's position in party development is the association they make between Madison and the antiparty rhetoric of *Federalist* 10.

Nevertheless, it would be a mistake to consider the arguments Madison made in the heat of the constitutional battle to be his most complete or final reflections on this or any other topic. Madison's party editorials from the 1790s—his most extensive works on the nature and purpose of political parties—revealed both differences from and similarities to his early party utterances. The opening paragraph in Madison's essay "A Candid State of Parties" is helpful on this point.

> As it is the business of the contemplative statesman to trace the history of parties in a free country, so it is the duty of the citizen at all times to understand the actual state of them. Whenever this duty is omitted, an opportunity is given to designing men, by the use of artificial or nominal distinctions, to oppose and balance against each other those who never differed as to the end to be pursued, and may no longer differ as to the means of attaining it.[5]

Quite possibly, the first sentence in the above quotation explains the difference between Madison's writings in 1789 and in 1792; Publius may have been a "contemplative statesman" and these later works the product of a responsible "citizen." The distinction between the role of the statesman and the role of a citizen is consistent with much of the classical literature in political philosophy. The Madisonian statesman was involved in founding a new regime and the Madisonian citizen was involved in perpetuating an existing regime. By making this distinction, Madison echoed sentiments expressed in Plato's *Republic*, Aristotle's *Politics*, and Machiavelli's *Prince*, and he anticipated the observation made so forcefully by Abraham Lincoln in his speech to the Young Men's Lyceum in 1838.[6]

Madison's works as a responsible citizen must be viewed with yet another factor in mind. The central theme of his famous *Federalist* 10 argument was that the newly proposed Constitution would lessen the violent effects of faction. If his argument proved correct, then factions would be less dangerous to our political life once the Constitution was the working blueprint for America, which it became by the 1790s.

With the constitutional safeguards against the violence of faction in place, Madison could talk about the parties of his day as "an experienced and dispassionate observer."[7] One of the distinguishing characteristics of this discussion versus the one found in *The Federalist* is that Madison identified two distinct parties; he no longer referred to a multiplicity of interests or sects. The three distinct party periods he cited further reflected a maturing party system. The issues surrounding these later party conflicts were more refined and more sophisticated.

Madison may have exaggerated the extent to which he was a dispassionate observer of the party battle, but by the 1790s he certainly was an experienced party observer. His description of the two national parties as the Republican and Antirepublican parties (he capitalized only "Republican") denied his opponents their more common title of Federalists. What is more important to our current investigation is Madison's description of the Republican party:

> The Republican party, as it may be termed, conscious that the mass of people in every part of the union, in every state, and in every occupation must at bottom be with them, both in interest and sentiment, will naturally find their account in burying all antecedent questions, in banishing every other distinction than that between enemies and friends to republican government, and in promoting a general harmony among the latter, wherever residing, or however employed.[8]

Compare this description to the one he gave of a faction in *Federalist* 10.

> By a faction I understand a number of citizens, whether amounting to a majority or minority of the whole, who are united and actuated by some common impulse of passion, or of interest, adverse to the rights of other citizens, or to the permanent and aggregate interests of the community.

The former statement describes a more refined and enlightened organization. Such a refined and enlightened organization was, no doubt, made possible by the establishment of institutional safeguards found in the Constitution. This is precisely what Madison had maintained throughout *The Federalist*. What did not change within Madison's political perspective was his confidence in the new science of politics as a primary protector of republican liberty. In fact, a careful reading of his party editorials reveals no fundamental change in his faith in the new science of politics.

Surprisingly little has been written about Madison's collection of party essays. What has been written on these essays has dealt more with Madison's political history or thought than with the essays' importance as the starting point of America's partisan life.[9] Madison's party essays could be as important to understanding America's party founding as *The Federalist* is to understanding America's constitutional founding.

Madison's notes for the *National Gazette* essays provide a wonderful insight into his political attitudes and beliefs at the time he was formulating the ideas that would be the foundation for America's first opposition movement.[10] The Madisonian citizen was still guided by the same basic political principles that guided the Madisonian statesman.

> The best provision for a stable and free Govt. is not a balance in the powers of the Govt. tho' that is not to be neglected, but an equilibrium in the interests & passions of the Society itself, which can not be attained in a small Society. Much has been said on the first. The last deserves a thorough investigation.[11]

In the next note he continued:

> The larger the community, the more respectable the whole & the less the share of importance felt by each member—the more submissive consequently each individual to the general will.[12]

The echoes of *Federalist* 10 can easily be heard in both these notes.

The notes he made when preparing for his essay on "Government of the United States" reveal a similar parallel to his arguments in *Federalists* 39 and 51:

> Here is the most characteristic trait in the Govt. on the U.S.—The powers surrendered by the people of America, are divided into two parts, one for the State, the other for the Genl. Govt. & each subdivided into Legislative Ex. & Judiciary. As in a single Govt. the Legislative Ex. & Judicy. ought to be kept separate by defensive armour for each. So ought the two Govts. federal and State.[13]

With his basic political principles still firmly in place, the Madisonian citizen's behavior appeared to be guided by changes in circumstance only. Madison's progression from founding to perpetuating is a better explanation for his thrust in the 1790s than any claim that he abandoned his earlier "soberminded reflections."[14]

The party structure developed in the 1790s was designed to strengthen the legislative branch of government. With the Federalists firmly in control of the executive branch (especially after Jefferson's resignation from Washington's cabinet), the opposition forces found Capitol Hill to be the best place for their early activities. While there are numerous theories about the initial cause or causes of the first partisan division in American politics,[15] it must be observed that it was largely a struggle between the different branches of government. The importance of organization and shared strategies is one of the concluding themes of "A Candid State of Parties":

> Whether the republican or the rival party will ultimately establish its ascendance, is a problem which may be contemplated now; but which time alone can solve. On one hand experience shews that in politics as in war, stratagem is often a overmatch for numbers.[16]

Madison's letters during this period indicated how actively he was working on "stratagem."[17]

The base of the Republican party's power was almost as important as the arguments it advanced. The *National Gazette* articles Madison wrote in 1791 and 1792 made as strong a case for the most populous branch of government as they did for Republican policies. Madison's partisan maneuvers must be recognized for what they were: he was practicing in the 1790s what he had preached in the 1780s. His efforts at organizing congressional opposition to the strong executive initiatives taken by Alexander Hamilton were a textbook example of the power struggles he described in *Federalist* 51. He truly believed that "ambition must be made to counteract ambition."

Madison has often been accused of theoretical inconsistencies and policy reversals,[18] but his policy reversals, such as they were, may have been the result of his theoretical consistencies.[19] This is as true of his position on political parties as it is in any other area.[20]

The Republican party takes on special significance if we keep in mind that it was a congressional party, first and foremost. Madison developed the party to strengthen the ability of Congress to check executive power—a task the party performed admirably. Even after Jefferson's election to the presidency in 1800, the Republican party continued to be a check on the presidency. This continued control was best exemplified by the development of congressional caucuses as nominating committees for presidential candidates.

The close executive-legislative relations that existed for the next twenty years are easy to understand in the light of congressional nomination of presidential candidates. But the next generation of political leaders was just as uncomfortable with the appearance of congressional dominion as Madison had been with the appearance of executive dominion. For this reason the second generation of political leaders developed America's executive party structure. This was accomplished when presidential nomination conventions replaced the old Congressional (or King) Caucus. With this transition, true national party organizations were developed. Presidential nominating conventions were integral to the development of grass-roots party organizations. Prior to this development there were no national party organizations outside of Congress.

Andrew Jackson was the symbolic leader of the move to create an executive party system, but the true architect for this stage of party development was Van Buren. While there are a few works that recognize Van Buren's role in party development in America, the full importance of his contribution is largely ignored.[21] Simply stated, he was as important to the development of presidential parties as Madison was to the development of congressional parties.

Van Buren was the first and most comprehensive advocate of national political parties as grass-roots campaign organizations. Unfortunately, his political history has received more attention than his political theory. He developed a sound theory for political parties in his much neglected work *The Origin and Course of Political Parties in the United States*. This work was the first detailed and most comprehensive break from the antiparty sentiments expressed by the founding generation.

There are two important aspects of the development of presidential parties which must be noted. First, this second stage of party development was different from the first stage because it focused on the executive branch of government. Nevertheless, this second stage was similar to the first stage of party development in that it strengthened our constitutional system of separation of powers. The primary shortcoming of all major works on the origin and development of America's party system lies in the failure of those works to recognize this second and most fundamental point.

Party reformers over the past century have all been either blind or hostile to this most basic aspect of eighteenth-century political parties in America. It is this ignorance or intentional redirection of party energies that has led to most if not all of the confusion that surrounds the importance and purpose of political parties today.

Party reformers have shared some common characteristics. The most destructive of these has been their desire to use party reforms as a vehicle to get around "constitutional inconveniences." The chief "inconvenience" has been the very system of separation of powers our parties were founded to maintain. While the methods used by reformers have varied, their ends have been fairly consistent.

The auxiliary precautions Madison defended in *The Federalist* (especially 47 and 51) as a primary check against tyranny have been pushed aside by reformers as unnecessary obstacles to true democracy. Whether this is due to mass communication, a more generally educated public, or the development of organized national parties, reformers have argued that our constitutional system of separation of powers is an ancient relic of a bygone era. All of these reform movements have demonstrated a clear hostility to the very constitutional safeguard that parties were originally developed to protect.

The understanding our first two generations of political leaders possessed about the philosophical foundations of a free society has been abandoned by reformers who want a "quick fix" solution to all our political problems. The other aspect of the founders' scheme that these reformers seem willing, if not eager, to abandon is the notion of a limited government.

Party reformers have taken a wide range of approaches to deal with the perceived shortcomings of our constitutional system. Some, like the Progressives, seem to dislike the restraints that have been placed on the will of the majority. As will be demonstrated, they feel that constitutional checks and balances were designed to thwart the majority will. For this reason, they argue that the Constitution and the traditional political party system were anti-majoritarian.

In contrast, the factional reformers who have dominated the Democratic party since 1968 have argued that the traditional party system, like the Constitution, has demonstrated a lack of interest in the needs of minority groups. These reformers appear hostile to the constitutional arrangements that were designed to curb the "violence of faction." For this group, the unleashing of factions is the best way to advance democracy.

These two groups use some surprisingly similar rhetoric to accomplish radically different results. Yet both claim to be advocates of true democracy. The Democratic party has continued to be the main battleground for these conflicting interests. The victories the factional reformers—the people who seem to have dominated the Democratic party commissions—have enjoyed over the past quarter of a century have kept them out of the White House for all but four years during that period.

The Democratic Leadership Council, a progressive-minded group once headed by Bill Clinton, has started a counterassault on the factional reformers.[22] Only time will reveal the outcome of this internal battle. What is clear at this point is that with the progressive reformers lies the Democrats' best hope to become a viable presidential party again. Clinton's election was a positive sign for progressive Democrats, but his cabinet appointments gave them little reason to rejoice.

A third group of reformers has been active over the past century as well. This group may best be labeled the responsible party advocates. While they have met with less success than the other groups, they have been the most enduring. They are clearly the most hostile to separation of powers. The methods they have advocated have changed from time to time but their message has not. They want parties to become the dominant policy-makers in our governmental system so they can be held responsible at election time. Some of these reformers want us to switch to a straight parliamentary system; others believe a more centralized party system is all that is called for.

Either way, responsible party reformers think every election should be a referendum on the party in power, and separation of powers often makes it difficult to determine who is in power. The responsible party reformers are closer to the progressive reformers than the factional reformers because they desire a clearer determination of the majority will.

All of these reformers desire a political system that is more centralized and more comprehensive than the system created by the Constitution or the founders of America's two-party system. They recognize that the majority of American citizens have a strong attachment to the Constitution and the political system that has evolved out of that document. For this reason, these reformers have always been a distinct minority in America, which has made packaging their reforms—to make our system more democratic—especially difficult.

Party reformers provide an interesting insight into different theoretical perspectives that have existed and do exist in America. Their lack of understanding of or appreciation for the work of our constitutional founders reveals just how much insight and foresight the founding generation possessed—an insight that was shared by the founders of America's two-party system. Our constitutional founders understood what was needed to make a democratic system of government work, but the system they created was not perfect. The development of political parties helped improve our constitutional system. The party founders were able to improve our political system because they accepted the theoretical assumptions that were built into the Constitution.

Political reformers who have accepted the basic principles of the Constitution and have truly attempted to reform and improve on that system have enjoyed considerable success. Those "reformers" who have not accepted the fundamental principles of our constitutional system have not. Political parties were created to be guardians of our constitutional system of separation of powers. Reformers who fail to recognize this fact are not reformers at all; they are deformers who want to destroy the very principles that have allowed our system to succeed.

A clear understanding of these party "reformers" requires that we look at the history of party reform efforts over the past century. The three major party reform efforts during this period have been championed by the progressive reformers (the antiparty reformers), the responsible reformers (the constitutional party reformers), and the commission reformers (the factional party reformers). Each of these reform movements has grown out of a different set of circumstances and each has approached reform in a slightly different way, but in the final analysis, each has proved to be very detrimental to our two-party system and to the Constitution our party system was originally set up to protect.

The first of these reforms was an overt attack on the existing national parties. This attack received its clearest and most complete expression in the pages of *The New Republic* and in the Progressive party's critique of the Republican and Democratic parties. Many Progressives did not abandon the established parties and worked for reform from within those organizations. The second wave of reforms was packaged as a nonpartisan effort. The high point of this effort, if there was one, was the publication by the Committee on Political Parties of the American Political Science Association of "Toward a More Responsible Two-Party System" (1950). A lengthy debate ensued, largely among academics, and then the issue seemed to die out until its revival by two groups: the Committee on Party Renewal (1976) and the Committee on the Constitutional System (1982). The third wave of reforms has been focused primarily within the Democratic party. The McGovern-Fraser Commission of 1968 was one of the first in what appears to be an unending series of commissions set up to restructure the delegate selection process for the Democratic presidential nominating conventions.

As one might guess, reforms in one party have a ripple effect on the other, so some of the Democratic party's reforms have altered the rules of the party nomination game for both parties. At first glance, these reforms do not appear to be as hazardous for the Republicans as they have been for the Democrats. But the jury is still out. In the long run, it is hard to imagine that the weakening of either party is to the advantage of the overall system.

Despite their differences on the surface, I believe there is a common thread connecting all three of these reform efforts: the abandonment of our constitutional system of checks and balances. The rhetoric of reform wants us to believe that the passage of time, the growth of our nation, industrial expansion, or modern technology has made our old constitutional system obsolete—that further democratization requires that we free ourselves from the shackles of this eighteenth-century document. But common sense and hindsight make it clear that all of these reformers have lacked the very qualities that made our founding fathers' work timeless:

an understanding of human nature and an appreciation for the limits of
government. Both of these helped the founders understand the importance
of separation of powers.

George Carey has observed that while there are many areas of dispute
related to the founding of the American regime, the central importance of
separation of powers to the founding enterprise is beyond question.

> We can say without fear of contradiction, however, that its framers were
> convinced beyond any doubt that separation of powers was absolutely neces-
> sary for a just and stable political order; indeed, a separation of powers ranks
> as the most fundamental of our constitutional principles.[23]

This point, which is developed more fully in Chapter 4, is critical to a clear
understanding of the total American political system. The importance of
separation of powers goes beyond the usual understanding of it as an integral part of checks and balances. Separation of powers is desirable because
it also "makes the powers work better."[24] Harvey Mansfield Jr. makes a
convincing case for this second point becoming of greater importance to
Publius in the latter papers of *The Federalist*. The party systems created
by Madison and Van Buren further enhanced the efficiency of the different
popular branches.

The failure of party reform movements over the past century is a direct
result of the reformers' inability to understand that political parties were
initially designed to strengthen, not weaken, our constitutional system.
Reforms that are hostile to the Constitution are doomed to failure because,
contrary to the beliefs of Woodrow Wilson and E. E. Schattschneider,
parties did not replace the Constitution as the dominant framework for our
system of government. In fact, political parties have had their greatest
failures when they have attempted to do that very thing.

By examining these reform efforts, we can better understand the true
and proper role of political parties within the American political system,
a role that has always been and must continue to be subservient to the
Constitution.

Because of this focus, the following study is not intended to be either a
historical account of political parties or a survey of the literature on political parties. What is intended is an examination of party reform efforts that
pays special attention to the reformers' theoretical assumptions about the
nature of democracy and the Constitution.

For this reason, this volume is broken down into four parts which do
not follow any neat chronological order. Chapters 1 and 2 focus on progressive reformers, Chapters 3 and 4 on responsible reformers, Chapters 5
and 6 on commission reformers, and the Conclusion examines all of these
efforts in the light of our constitutional system and the theoretical principles at the heart of that system.

Chapter One

Progressive Assault

Of the three reform groups cited, the Progressives were clearly the most ambitious and the most hostile toward political parties. Progressives desired sweeping reforms in American society, and while their means were largely political, their ends were social and economic. The political system they inherited from the founders was too limited for their purposes. As Samuel Duncan-Clark explained in *The Progressive Movement*, Theodore Roosevelt revealed this feeling when he described the progressive movement as

> the intelligent expression of a popular protest; it is the instrument of the people's aspiration for a larger economic, social and political life; it is the acknowledgment that our progress has been unequal from the ethical, political and industrial standpoints, so that our governmental clothes need to be changed and enlarged to fit our increased bodily growth, our increasing and changing economic needs.[1]

The two obstacles that stood in the way of changing and enlarging our "governmental clothes," at the national level, were the Constitution and the two-party system. Despite the efforts of scholars like Charles Beard and J. Allen Smith, the Constitution continued to be greatly revered by most Americans, leaving political parties to receive the brunt of the Progressives' attack.

Political parties were not the focus of reform simply because they were the easier prey. Another belief that existed at the turn of the century, and is common among some reformers yet today, was that political parties, in an important sense, replaced our constitutional system of 1787. Perpetuating such a myth served reformers in two ways. First, their attack on political parties can be presented as a way of returning to the founders' faith. Second, if parties have already replaced the founders' system, what the Progressives were advocating was no more radical than what occurred

13

during the Jacksonian era. *The New Republic* described this political transformation:

> The two parties really became the government because they constituted the
> only effective organization of the electorate for the accomplishment of politi-
> cal purposes. But they formed an unofficial and irresponsible government
> which gradually ceased to be popular, and which made all movements pay
> tribute to the idols of Democracy and Republicanism and their priests.[2]

This assertion is wrong on two fundamental points. First, political parties never became the government. They recruited personnel for the government and they worked hard at trying to influence the government, but
they were not the government. Their failure to see this is the result of many
Progressives' inability to distinguish between government and politics. In
Federalist 15 we find a simple and direct definition of government: "Government implies the power of making laws." The Constitution grants this
power to the Congress. Politics plays a major role in determining who will
be represented in the Congress but, by law, only members of Congress
have the power to cast votes for and against new laws. It should be noted
that what the Progressives were describing is precisely what the next set
of party reformers are prescribing. Second, the Progressives' belief that
the two major political parties had "ceased to be popular" has been
proved wrong by the march of time. Both the Democratic and Republican
parties, though weakened and battered, are still with us today.

There was not unanimous consent among the Progressives as to what
specific reforms were needed but, generally, they called for presidential
primaries; greater use of initiative, referendum, and recall; and the direct
election of senators. While initiatives, referendum, and recalls never
caught on at the national level, they have enjoyed considerable though
somewhat erratic success at the state and local levels. These proposals
may not seem terribly radical to us today, in part because of the extent of
the Progressives' success in implementing their program. What is important for us to keep in mind is the extent to which these proposals weakened
our party system. Let us look at presidential primaries and why this was
one of the key reforms of the era.

Progressives disliked political parties for many reasons but the one most
often cited was that parties were preservers of privilege. The greatest sym-
bol of party privilege was believed to be the party convention. Students of
American history know that party conventions were created, at the national level, to replace the old King Caucus. But Progressives felt that
party conventions were every bit as corrupt and undemocratic as the caucuses had been:

The convention system was based upon the theory that there is superior wisdom in delegated assemblies. That theory no longer applies to politics, and the system itself has become the convenient tool of bosses, machines and special interests. Committees on credentials and resolutions do most of the work in conventions; a compact organization, with a chairman trained in tactics and indifferent to criticism or protest, can turn a convention into a body of subservient puppets, or can create a majority where none existed, that will run rough-shod over the will of the people. The term ''steam-roller'' grew out of the convention system as a picturesque description of the ruthless methods employed by bosses and machines.[3]

The Progressives' solution to this problem was the solution they posed for most problems in American society—greater democracy. As Duncan-Clark explained:

The direct primary places in the hands of the people the right and the power to name their candidates for office. It greatly lessens the peril of boss rule and strikes a crushing blow at the alliance between professional politics and privilege.[4]

Roosevelt probably summed up the Progressive mood best when he stated, ''The power of the people must be made supreme within the several party organizations.''[5]

The Progressive scheme called for a fairly direct link between the voting public and their elected representatives. The closer that tie, the less need there would be for political parties. Roosevelt seemed to envision the Progressive party as permanently what Thomas Jefferson's Republican party had been temporarily: becoming the party to end all parties. This was possible because, according to most Progressive literature, the goal of the enlightenment had finally been fulfilled. Duncan-Clark captured this article of faith when he proclaimed:

Today knowledge is widely diffused. Schools, colleges and universities have raised the average of intelligence. Fast mail, telegraphs and telephones link every corner of the country and narrow the world to small compass. Thousands of newspapers keep the people informed; scores of magazines carry on an invaluable work of education. Free libraries, chautauquas and innumerable organizations devoted to the discussion of social, economic and political questions provoke study and reflection.[6]

The kind of public leadership political parties had performed had been obviated by mass education and rapid communication. What had actually happened was that mass communication and rapid transportation had, once again, strengthened the ability of individuals to make direct appeals to the public. As had happened in the 1820s, America was once again faced with the alternative between a system dominated by party leadership and one dominated by personal leadership. Roosevelt's vision of the alternative is ably described during the 1910 campaign:

> The leader holds his position, purely because he is able to appeal to the conscience and to the reason of those who support him, and the boss holds his position because he appeals to fear of punishment and hope of reward. The leader works in the open, the boss in covert. The leader leads, and the boss drives.[7]

But these were not the only two options available. In addition to the independent political leader Roosevelt described, there were party leaders whose appeal was to more than the national conscience and who—at the same time—were not the entrenched bosses whose appeal was primarily monetary. Progressives were almost unanimous in their praise of Jefferson and Abraham Lincoln, two of America's premier party leaders.

In the preface to Duncan-Clark's book on the progressive movement, Roosevelt criticized the Republican party for abandoning the original principles of Lincoln and the Democratic party for losing sight of Jefferson's original intentions. The Progressives' reverence for Lincoln and Jefferson as America's most inspirational statesmen was well placed. Harry Jaffa has argued that their greatness was due, at least in part, to their ability to transcend the usual political rhetoric. Here is how he described one component of this:

> Lincoln once said that public opinion on any subject always had a central idea from which all its minor thoughts radiated. Lincoln's political genius lay, not in finding a common denominator of the differing demands of his multi-group coalition, but in finding the *one* demand that was at the center of them all. Or, to be still more precise, it was to articulate in its full meaning the one thought—the equality of all men—which lay at the bottom of that one demand.[8]

But their greatness was not due exclusively to their intellectual genius or their rhetorical gifts. Jefferson and Lincoln's philosophical understanding of the "central idea" of American society—the notion that "all men are created equal"—was in need of an institutional anchor, and they both recognized party machinery as the best institution to provide that anchor. Roosevelt's scheme sounds too much like some Weberian plan for institutionalizing charisma. Appealing to the conscience of a people, as Roosevelt suggested, can be done by a Hitler as easily as a Lincoln.

Maintaining the "central idea" of this or any other regime requires a system that accommodates the ambition of "the family of lions, or the tribe of the eagle," to use Lincoln's terminology, but at the same time forces those ambitions to perpetuate the "central idea." As long as political parties are the vehicles through which those ambitions are channeled, the principles that guided the party in past generations will impose limits on the passions of future generations. Lincoln succeeded because he refrained from appealing to the "conscience" of the people as the abolitionists did; instead, he chose the safer and nobler ground of the founders' faith—a faith that may have been less pure, in the abstract theoretical sense, but one that was politically consistent with both the means and the ends employed by the founders. For this reason, Lincoln's ambition—like Jefferson's before him—was tempered by the desire to perpetuate our political institutions. This was the message of Lincoln's speech to the Young Men's Lyceum, a message our twentieth-century party reformers have failed to understand.

There is a subtle, yet critical, distinction here that must not be overlooked. Appeals to conscience can be purely passionate; appeals to an idea must be guided ultimately by reason. As was illustrated in Plato's *Republic*, there are times when direct appeals to reason will be unsuccessful if they do not make some concession to the strong passions we all harbor. Jaffa illustrated this very point when he described the challenge that confronted Lincoln as he wrestled with his own political ambition:

> The task of a leader is to find a point of coincidence between the moral demands which are dear to the men he would lead and their self-interests, and to turn this, not only against the unjust self-interests of others, but the unjust self-interests of his followers. The popular leader must be prepared to gratify the less-than-noble but not immoral demands of his would-be supporters if he is to have their support for the higher purposes of statesmanship. To hold these meaner services in contempt is to abandon popular government to those who have only mean ends, and to make of popular government a mean thing. Men may be led toward higher purposes of which they are scarcely conscious, if those who hold these purposes first show concern for and an ability to gratify their less noble demands.[9]

This is why appeals to conscience without some understanding of the ultimate goal of a political regime can be dangerously misleading.

The Progressives broke from the faith of both Jefferson and Lincoln in a more radical way than had either of the two major parties. Unlike their predecessors from the Era of Good Feeling, the Progressives knew that party leadership had historic ties to the existing constitutional system. A major appeal of personal leadership was that it permitted greater freedom from constitutional restraints, freedom that would ultimately permit the growth of executive power and the weakening of the archaic system of checks and balances. If the Progressive reforms succeeded, the immediate losers would be the legislatures and the established political parties.

Whatever differences may have existed between Roosevelt and Woodrow Wilson, the two men were in theoretical agreement on the question of leadership. Wilson's *The Study of Public Administration* presents a commonly held Progressive view on America's political development. With the Civil War, America had settled its last real political dispute. All that was left for Americans to do was to clean up the machinery of government. This was primarily an administrative task and is also why executive functions were being shifted to administrative officers.

In the eyes of the Progressives, government had moved from the realm of the political to the realm of the technical. Party functionaries were no longer needed; bureaucrats were. *The New Republic* captured this opinion in a 1914 essay titled "The Future of the Two-Party System":

> The American democracy will not continue to need the two-party system to intermediate between the popular will and the governmental machinery. By means of executive leadership, expert administrative independence and direct legislation, it will gradually create a new governmental machinery which will be born with the impulse to destroy the two-party system, and will itself be thoroughly and flexibly representative of the underlying purposes and needs of a more social democracy.[10]

Notice how cleverly this is phrased: "a new governmental machinery" based on "executive leadership, expert administrative independence and direct legislation," all of which, the author believed, would obviate our two-party system. But the two-party system was not all that was being threatened. This new governmental machinery was a direct assault on our constitutional system as well.

Herbert Croly provided the most thorough and complete theoretical justification for this "new governmental machinery." As an author and publisher, Croly had the luxury of taking a more extreme position than did the active Progressive politicians. Yet he was not the most radical of the Progressive theorists. He had positive, well-developed ideas about the nature and direction of the progressive movement.

Croly's book *Progressive Democracy* is especially good on the topic of political parties. He considered political parties to be a necessary part of the inevitable transition our government must make as it moved from a representative system dominated by law to a more mature progressive democracy dominated by public opinion. Like Duncan-Clark, Croly believed that mass opinion had advanced to the point where it could and should assume its rightful place as the guiding force in our political system.

Croly, in typical progressive fashion, argued that our society had evolved and surpassed the old political system which he characterized as a "monarchy of Law." He believed America's old constitutional system would be "confronted and superseded by a new system—the result of an alert social intelligence as well as an aroused individual conscience."[11]

Political parties had performed an important service during this developmental period, but they needed to make way for the new, more democratic vehicle of public opinion. Croly further believed that the efforts to reform the two-party system exposed the true limitations of that system:

> If the two-party system is breaking down as an agency for democratizing an undemocratic government, the remedy is not to democratize the party which was organized to democratize the government, but to democratize the government itself.[12]

The development of initiative, referendum, recall, and primaries was necessary but not sufficient means for democratizing our political system. Another key ingredient would be to make the political system more executive centered. Croly's plan for making the executive the true transmitter of public opinion had characteristics quite similar to the arguments advanced by the responsible reformers.

What attracted Croly to executive leadership over party leadership were many of the very qualities that pushed Martin Van Buren in the opposite direction. Van Buren preferred party loyalty over personal loyalty because it brought greater stability to the political system. Van Buren also knew that parties would build their constituents' loyalty around political principles—principles that were guided and illuminated by our constitutional system. James Ceaser described Van Buren's "ideal leader" as little more than a political "broker."[13] Croly felt the tendency of parties to reinforce constitutional principles was the very attribute that kept them from advancing true democracy. This was what permitted Croly to praise the two-party system as "the most effective method which has yet been devised for the organization of majority rule" and still condemn parties because they "can never get away from the initial vice of being no more than an attempt to democratize a group of undemocratic political institutions."[14]

The new executive envisioned by Croly was to become the center of our political system. As the sole representative of the entire nation, the executive is the only person who can truly represent majority opinion. One of the chief advantages of an executive-centered democracy is that it must be built around programs, not principles. Croly liked this shift because majorities built around programs are more fleeting and temporary than those built around principles. An executive subject to recall would be far more sensitive to popular opinion than any other person or institution under a system based on cumbersome constitutional law.

Croly's new progressive executive was not simply a follower of mass opinion. Quite the contrary, the central task of this new executive was to personalize and enliven public opinion: "Strong individual leadership supplies popular opinion with a needed mental and moral tonic." Democratic societies, even progressive democratic societies, need an agent to translate their "vague popular aspirations" into specific programs. The role of a progressive executive went beyond mere policy formation as well: "Even the most sophisticated societies are rarely able to feel much enthusiasm about a principle or a program until it becomes incarnated in a vivid personality and is enhanced as a result of the incarnation."[15]

With the emancipation of the popular will through a strong and responsive executive some additional changes would be needed. One of these was the restructuring of our administrative state. According to Croly, an additional shortcoming of the old two-party system was its hostility toward administrative departments. The new system called for restructuring the agencies so they could become additional tools of democracy.

As the executive's task becomes more representative and less administrative, stronger administrative departments will be needed. But they will have to do more than just pick up duties previously performed by the executive.

The new progressive administrators will also take over many of the functions previously performed by the two-party system. The old party-run government used administrative positions as rewards for faithful party workers. If these "administrators" were not terribly efficient or knowledgeable about their jobs no one seemed to care. After all, they had the job because of what they had already done, not because of any expectation over what they would do.

The new progressive administrators would change all this. First, they would be administering programs that had clear popular support. As our government becomes more policy-oriented, the efficient administration of these policies will be more critical. The new progressive executive will be judged on his ability to deliver on his promises. This will force executives to appoint administrators who are knowledgeable about specific policy areas and have the necessary managerial skills to run agencies efficiently. Blind loyalty to a political party will no longer be enough to secure an important governmental job.

The second characteristic of the new progressive administrator would be allegiance and acceptance of the new social programs. Administrators who have this social consciousness can be given significant latitude in their administrative responsibilities. Croly would grant the "conscientious and competent administrator of an official social program" the same degree of independence and authority that was traditionally granted to common law judges. He viewed these administrators as custodians of "a social purpose of which the law is only a fragmentary expression."

> As the custodian of a certain part of the social program, he must share the faith upon which the program depends for its impulse; and he must accept the scientific method upon which the faith depends for its realization. Thus with all his independence he is a promoter and propagandist.[16]

With this amazing mixture of scientific management and progressive faith, these new super administrators will go out and propagandize the newly enlightened and conscientious public.

An intriguing and unusual union takes place in Croly's discussion of the new progressive administrator. It is a union, as we will see in later chapters, that is only hinted at by Roosevelt and Wilson. The expectations many people had for scientific management and methods had become almost commonplace at this time. The statements cited earlier by Duncan-Clark and Croly on the greater role human reason could and should play in our political and social lives were at the very heart of the progressive movement. This is why many Progressives believed that we, individually and collectively, had outgrown our need for such things as party allegiance and loyalty. One of Croly's great criticisms of political parties was that they enforced their discipline among members by cultivating artificial alliances. Most of these alliances were held together by emotional appeals based on loyalty to party symbols and historical appeals to party mythology.

And yet, Croly had no difficulty accepting a group of administrative propagandists who are moved by a similar kind of political faith. It is Croly's statements about the new progressive faith that appear ill-suited for the new progressive programs based on human reason and scientific methods. The progressive movement is not without its own appeals to emotional attachments, attachments that have very little to do with the cold calculations of the scientific revolution. Croly's discussions of the new progressive faith were a central component of his opposition to the old political system.

The new progressive faith is certainly a more forceful component in Croly's *Progressive Democracy* than it was in his earlier book, *The Promise of American Life*. His first book went to great lengths to develop a progressive history of the United States; his second book relied more on an expression of progressive faith. In 1909 an elaborate history was needed to develop his thesis; by 1914 he felt he could get by with a statement of progressive faith.

Croly seemed to think that this faith was a necessary substitute for law. In fact, the chapter where he developed this notion is appropriately titled "The Law and The Faith." In this chapter Croly contended: "A democracy becomes courageous, progressive and ascendent just insofar as it dares to have faith, and just insofar as it can be faithful without ceasing to be inquisitive." Croly added that, like the Christian faith, this is faith in the "unseen and unknown." As this faith grows, the need for laws diminishes proportionately.[17]

An exact definition of this faith is not easily extracted from Croly's writings. At one point it is described as a "social ideal" that must be advanced by a "social will."[18] Croly seemed to use the terms social, national, and collective interchangeably when he discussed this all-important will. In a later chapter he argued: "The national will has the responsibility of being the custodian and the creator instead of the servant of the national ideal."[19]

In the final analysis, Croly's progressive faith rested with a certain kind of popular will. He acknowledged throughout this discussion the new emerging relationship between individualism and collectivism. Should that relationship continue to evolve and mature, our heightened sense of social responsibility will obviate laws and institutions designed to check our baser ambitions and passions. Or, as he asserted: "Thus the progressive democratic faith, like the faith of St. Paul, finds its consummation in a love which is partly expressed in sympathetic feeling, but which is at bottom a spiritual expression of the mystical unity of human nature."[20]

The simplest way to describe this new progressive faith would appear to be the following: we should abandon the political philosophy of John Locke for the political philosophy of Jean-Jacques Rousseau. Instead of protecting our basic or natural rights by constitutional laws and auxiliary precautions, we should be striving for our natural perfectibility by freeing our socially educated wills. Under this system, the executive becomes a progressive evangelist who personifies the progressive faith and the administrators become something like seminar leaders who show the masses how to apply that faith to their daily lives.

To Croly's credit, he did not ignore the risks involved in his progressive leap of faith. He mentioned again and again that there are considerable risks involved in this scheme. But he also believed that there were risks involved if we failed to seize this occasion:

Risks must be incurred. It is only a matter of degree. Politics is so far from being an exact science that plausible prudential reasons can be urged against any experiment; but such reasons are not and cannot be conclusive. If our knowledge of politics does not permit us to predict the success of a thorough-going democratic experiment, neither does it permit us to prophesy its fail-ure. We have a right to be skeptical of any attempt to reduce political theory to a science of causes and effects.[21]

He follows this statement with one of his most emphatic and revealing utterances. For him, a "thoroughgoing democracy is not to be prophesied. It is to be created; and in the process of creation an uncompromising faith in the moral value of democracy is the essential thing."

At this point there can be little doubt that the heart and soul of the progressive movement, in Croly's eyes at least, was the rejection of all past attempts to come to a reasonable understanding of human nature; we must stop reasoning and start creating. Reason, like institutions, ties us to our past in very restrictive ways; faith and creativity liberate us from our past so we can fulfill the promise of our future. By letting "progressive democratic faith" be our "primary creative agency" we will become op-ponents of authoritarian intellectualism and allies of pragmatism.[22]

Of course there is the more practical side of the progressive movement to which we must return. But the theoretical component we just explored must be kept in mind because it is an important force behind progressive actions. Whether the active progressive politicians fully understood or agreed with this progressive faith, it was always there as the theoretical justification and driving force behind their most radical reforms. Progres-sive faith was the foundation of this movement and the importance of this foundation was captured by Robert La Follette when he argued: "I have always felt that the political reformer, like the engineer or the architect, must know that his foundations are right. To build the superstructure in advance of that is likely to be disastrous to the whole thing."[23]

Within this context, we must view the passage of the Pendleton Act in 1883 as one small step for bureaucratic reform, one giant step for our new governmental system. But this new system could not be sold to the masses on the basis of a need to shift from Lockean theory to Rousseauean theory. Instead the reformers advanced their cause by focusing on more immediate and tangible concerns. David Thelen captured one aspect of this new atti-tude when he explained:

> To create a political system based on merit, these reformers constantly con-trasted the successful businessman with the successful politician. Measuring political performance against the yardstick of the businessman, these reform-ers concluded that partisanship was the basic problem of politics. The politi-cal system encouraged only the value of party loyalty, whereas the competi-tive world of business bred for talent, integrity, intelligence, and experience.

In contrast to businessmen who always had to reduce labor costs to remain competitive, politicians seemed ever eager to create unnecessary jobs—at great expense to taxpayers—to have places for the party's election workers. Since party loyalty was the only prerequisite for public employment, patronage appointees were generally incompetent and frequently corrupt, the reformer reasoned.[24]

Corruption, as we revealed above, was just the tip of the reformers' iceberg.

The shift away from party politics to bureaucratic politics—a term the reformers would not use—did not make government more efficient. With hindsight it is fairly clear that it had the opposite effect. The belief that government can function like a private business ignores the role competition plays in the marketplace. It also assumes that once bureaucratic agencies are in place, they will be above politics. One of the actual results of the movement away from party politics toward bureaucratic politics has been to change the location of the political battles. Under party politics most political battles are fought among the electorate; under bureaucratic politics these battles are fought in Congress or between Congress and the president.

This means that one of the main accomplishments of greater bureaucratization was (and is) that the public has become a little more isolated from political battles. This was not entirely by accident, but it does raise some serious questions about Progressives' appeals to and faith in the masses. Thelen argued that Progressive reforms "pointed in two very different directions: one toward democracy and another toward bureaucracy."[25] None of the leading Progressive thinkers considered these to be conflicting impulses. According to Roosevelt, La Follette, Croly, and other leading Progressive thinkers, the most immediate problem of American politics was corruption. And, on their horizon, democracy and bureaucracy were the quickest and best solutions to this problem. As we have already seen, democracy was perceived as the solution to corruption in the presidential nominating process. Bureaucratization would remove the patronage positions that institutionalized that corruption. Both of these moves were correctly perceived as attacks on the existing two-party system.

American politics had become fairly corrupt by the end of the nineteenth century, and America's two-party system was infected by this corruption. Yet the Progressive solution, to borrow a phrase from Madison, was a "remedy that was worse than the disease." The reformers, as they are described by Thelen, were wrong to assume that "partisanship was the basic problem of politics." If the problem was corruption and inefficiency, the two political parties were, as they had always been in American politics, a reflection of the larger system of which they were a part. Corruption was not a uniquely partisan phenomenon; corruption, as the reformers pointed out again and again, was as much a problem in business as it was in government. If it was not, then why were there so many complaints about the trusts, the railroads, and American industry at large? Upton Sinclair's *The Jungle* was no less damning of American industry than the muckrakers had been of American politics.

There were problems in America, but political parties were not the cause, they were one of the victims. The reason reformers were so eager to accuse parties and to attack them was that the progressive movement was, in the main, a movement of the educated upper-middle and upper classes. What these people disliked about political parties was their inability to control them. The urban machines were usually controlled by the ethnic groups that dominated the inner cities, and the national parties were usually controlled by an alliance between these urban (or, in some cases, state) machines and the heads of American industry. Neither of these groups had close ties to America's newly emerging educated professionals.[26]

By making American government more bureaucratic and technical, these educated professionals, as students of scientific management and technology, would bring the government closer to themselves. This was clearly a political move that did not, as its advocates claimed, depoliticize government, but simply altered the rules of the political game. There is no such thing as a politically neutral reform. Croly's plan for the new progressive administrators highlights this fact.

Not all reformers recognized this shift of power as a political ploy. Many of the reformers accepted the rhetoric of the movement at face value. It was hard to see that, by shifting the focus of American politics from the local party caucus or precinct meeting to some administrative office at the county or national seat of government, they were eroding the very fabric of our constitutional system. The twofold impact of this shift was to make the American political system considerably less democratic and profoundly more unitary. To put it another way, it made our political system much more like the one we found so obnoxious in 1776.

The moral to this story seems to be quite clear. The progressive movement failed because it never came to practical terms with the relationship between its means and its ends. The progressive movement was a movement obsessed with its social ends, and careful thought was not given to the means to achieving those ends. Progressives spoke eloquently about democracy and justice, and no doubt were sincere in their commitment to these principles. However, their extreme desire for democratic results made them too impatient to calculate carefully the appropriate means to achieve the desired results.

Earlier Thelen was cited claiming that the progressive movement pointed in two different directions: democracy and bureaucracy. Progressives saw these as a two-pronged attack on a single problem. The ideal end of progressive democracy was social justice; the minimal end of progressive bureaucracy was social control. Although democracy and bureaucracy may be of questionable compatibility as means, Progressives believed that the ends they would produce were quite compatible.

All the party reformers of this century have made a similar error. The responsible party reformers, like their predecessors, were (and are) obsessed with ends, whereas the commission reformers, as will be demonstrated, err in the opposite direction. Edward Banfield claimed that the commission reformers were so obsessed with democratic procedures or means that they completely ignored the results these procedures would produce. If the presidential elections since 1968 are any indication, American voters seem to agree with that assessment.

One of the great strengths of the founders was their careful consideration of both means and ends. The Declaration of Independence and the Preamble to the Constitution establish the highest ends possible for government; the rest of our Constitution and our two-party system provide the best means we know for achieving those ends. Reforms may be necessary from time to time, but our most successful reforms have always been those which move us closer to the ideals set forth by our founders, not those which claim to transcend them. Political parties may not have been endorsed by the founders, but they have done an excellent job of preserving the principles and institutions that were.

Lincoln provided some able guidance when he argued: "The people— the people—are the rightful masters of congresses, and courts—not to overthrow the constitution, but to overthrow the *men* who pervert it."[27]

Chapter Two

Theodore Roosevelt and Progressive Leadership

By 1912 it was clear that America's party system had disappointed Theodore Roosevelt. Some might argue that his disappointment began when he discovered that the Republican party had abandoned him for William Howard Taft. It may be more accurate to claim that his disappointment was the result of the party managers' cavalier attitude toward the will of the party electorate.

Regardless of the reasons for Roosevelt's change of heart toward the political parties of his day, his changed attitude toward America's party system was a turning point in presidential leadership in the United States—a change that had profound effect on America's national parties. Many of the changes in presidential style that are credited to Woodrow Wilson rightfully belong to Roosevelt. The most notable is the plebiscitary system of presidential selection.[1] This system, which permits a direct link between the presidential candidate and the voters, is precisely what Roosevelt was calling for when he made his appeal to Republican voters in 1912. His commitment to this system was well articulated when he defended presidential primaries before the Ohio Constitutional Convention on February 21, 1912:

> I believe in providing for direct nominations by the people, including therein direct preferential primaries for the election of delegates to the national nominating conventions. Not as a matter of theory, but as a matter of plain and proved experience, we find that the convention system, while it often records the popular will, is also often used by adroit politicians as a method of thwarting the popular will. In other words, the existing machinery for nominations is cumbrous, and is not designed to secure the real expression of the popular desire.[2]

Roosevelt's commitment to "the real expression of the popular desire" was not limited to presidential primaries or to political parties. To under-

27

stand fully the driving force behind his approach to leadership requires some further examination of the motives and expectations of the progressive movement, or at least that portion of the movement that he helped shape. As an active politician, Roosevelt was not given to rhetoric as extreme as what we examined in the previous chapter; nor were his desires for reforms. Roosevelt's candor and common sense may be the very things that separated him from the bulk of his Progressive allies. Nevertheless, he was no friend of the traditional parties by 1912; nor was he a great defender of the auxiliary precautions that were so dear to James Madison and the other constitutional founders.

Roosevelt's views on the nature and purpose of our two-party system and the constitutional system that shaped America's political parties must be examined. His reservations about both of these political institutions were presented in a more guarded fashion than were Herbert Croly's or those of a number of other writers for *The New Republic*. Yet his views grew out of the same era and were shaped by many of the same experiences; he was very much influenced by the Gilded Age. The events that produced the reform spirit in America were his clearest political memories as well.[3] Roosevelt was like most of his Progressive allies in that he was driven by a sincere and admirable optimism. What separated him from most other Progressives was the practical approach he took to applying his progressive beliefs. Where Croly discussed progressive faith, Roosevelt discussed progressive character. Croly's attitude toward people seemed motivated by his belief that they could be led; Roosevelt's attitude toward people seemed motivated by his belief in their basic decency.

The praise Thomas Jefferson had for the virtuous American farmers Roosevelt had for all Americans: "Our average fellow-citizen is a sane and healthy man, who believes in decency and has a wholesome mind." This, he believed, was why our democratic future was assured.[4] But there were forces of evil lurking in our society as well and it was incumbent on government to assure that they did not have an unfair advantage over the majority of Americans.

In this respect, Roosevelt was more traditional than Croly, Samuel Duncan-Clark, and many other Progressives. Croly seemed to place great faith in social engineering; Roosevelt had greater faith in human traits and sound character. They called for similar political reforms but the assumptions they made to justify and defend those changes were not the same. These differences have profound implications on their different understandings of the role and nature of leadership.

The differences that existed between Croly and Roosevelt in terms of their understanding of rights and obligations appear similar to the differences that existed between Jefferson and Abraham Lincoln. Like Jefferson, Croly focused most of his attention on establishing the rights citizens should possess. Like Lincoln, Roosevelt acknowledged these rights but placed considerable attention on the obligations that must accompany them. A cautionary note is needed, because Croly, like many of his Progressive allies, considered rights to be community based, not individually based. This is a limited but fitting analogy because no statesman was more highly regarded by either Roosevelt or Croly than Lincoln.

No one has developed this change of emphasis more clearly than Harry Jaffa in *Crisis of the House Divided*. His chapter on the Declaration of Independence presents one of the clearest and most insightful discussions of the relationship between rights and duties available. While it seems that the degree of difference was greater between Jefferson and Lincoln than it was between Croly and Roosevelt, Jaffa's argument is helpful in developing this point. The issue between Jefferson and Lincoln was the proper meaning and interpretation of "all Men are created equal." Jaffa's discussion begins by pointing out that the challenge that confronted Jefferson was different from the challenge confronting Lincoln: "Lincoln was trying to perpetuate a government, Jefferson in 1776 to overthrow one. . . ." But even after independence was achieved and our new constitutional system was in place, Jaffa observed: "Jefferson was always more concerned to remind the people of their rights than of their duties. He emphasized what they should demand of their government rather than what they must demand of themselves." Croly's writings have a similar emphasis.

Jaffa clearly saw more in the differences between Jefferson and Lincoln than mere historical circumstances; more important was their philosophical understanding of the proper relationship between the citizen and the state.

> Jefferson's horizon, with its grounding in Locke, saw all commands to respect the rights of others as fundamentally hypothetical imperatives: *if* you do not wish to be a slave, then refrain from being a master. Lincoln agreed, but he also said in substance: he who wills freedom for himself must simultaneously will freedom for others. Lincoln's imperative was not only hypothetical; it was categorical as well. Because all men by nature have an equal right to justice, all men have an equal duty to do justice, wholly irrespective of calculations as to self-interest.[5]

Accordingly, Lincoln's political morality is more than simply a quid pro quo. Lincoln's political morality is not based on Lockean principles; Jaffa described it as more dependent on Aristotle and Edmund Burke and, therefore, "a partnership 'in every virtue and in all perfection.' "[6] Lincoln's recognition that rights are not something passively granted by laws but must be actively pursued—if not earned—by citizens appealed to the prejudices of most Progressives. But Roosevelt had a keener sense of the full impact of this belief than did most of his fellow Progressives.

Croly assumed that Americans had achieved their right to move from a representative democracy dominated by laws to a progressive democracy dominated by their own desires and wants. According to Croly's historicism, once this point had been achieved, all that was required would be clarifying the rights that must be granted to those who have attained this level of political development. Roosevelt understood that citizens do not earn rights once and for all but have to demonstrate again and again that they understand and are willing to assume the duties that must accompany these rights.

Roosevelt's political morality was dependent on the character of the citizens. Rights are not historically determined; they are granted to people who demonstrate their ability and willingness to live lives worthy of the kind of political trust these rights demand. Nowhere is this made more clear than in his numerous references to good laws requiring good citizens. This is one of the most consistent themes expressed throughout his political life, but he never stated it more clearly than he did on the pages of *The Outlook* in 1911:

> We need good laws just as a carpenter needs good instruments. If he has no tools, the best carpenter alive cannot do good work. But the best tools will not make a good carpenter, any more than to give a coward a rifle will make him a good soldier. We wish to see the mass of our people move steadily upward to a higher social, industrial, and political level. To do this we wish to change the laws, and by this change to render it steadily easier for the right type of man, the right woman, to achieve better conditions. But unless the man and the woman are of the right type the laws can accomplish nothing. It rests within our own hands, it rests with us, the people of America, to determine our own fate; and character is the main factor in the determination. If betterment in social and industrial conditions means merely an increase in ease and sensual enjoyment, no good can permanently follow such betterment.[7]

Roosevelt did not end with his insistence on citizens' possessing sound democratic character. He pursued the issue further and more completely by also describing the virtues which constitute that character.

On this topic Roosevelt seemed every bit as Aristotelian as Jaffa's Lincoln. Roosevelt's moral democratic citizen must be honest, thrifty, hardworking, courageous, and efficient. But no mere listing of these qualities does justice to Roosevelt's image of the average American:

I believe that the average American citizen wishes nothing save what he can honestly obtain for himself by hard work and decent living. This is one reason why I so heartily believe in democracy. I believe in the future of the American people because I believe that fundamentally and at heart the average man and the average woman of America are sound; that, however deeply they may at times err, yet they have in them, fundamentally, the power of self-mastery, of self-control, the power to live their lives in accordance with a high and fine ideal, to do strict justice to others, and to insist upon their rights only as a vantage-point for the better performance of their duties.[8]

Being self-controlled and doing justice to others are the key elements of Roosevelt's democratic citizenship. He believed that this could be accomplished only if we control our "passions and appetites, and force head and hand to work according to the dictates of conscience."[9] The proper relationship between duties and rights was spelled out even more explicitly in his speech on "The Meaning of Free Government." The main theme of this speech was that self-government can occur only where the people have self-control: "I believe it is even more important for men to pay heed to their duties and to the rights of others than it is for them to pay heed to their own rights. But I believe also that they can only do their full duty when they enjoy fully their rights."[10]

In a truly democratic society, there is no alternative: either citizens recognize the rights of others or those rights will not exist. Rights and duties are so interdependent that it is foolhardy to discuss rights without acknowledging their dependence on duties. These are the inseparable Siamese twins of democratic citizenship; what makes them inseparable is that they are joined at the head, the heart, and the belly.

Understanding this relationship is central to understanding Roosevelt's views on progressive leadership. This is also why he placed so much emphasis on examples. One must lead a democratic people by both rhetoric and example. Roosevelt considered no one a more fitting example of democratic citizenship than Lincoln; his speeches were packed with references to Lincoln's words and deeds. Yet Lincoln was obviously a very uncommon citizen.

The way Lincoln led the nation was certainly important to Roosevelt. Lincoln was the catalyst for radical change, but more important for Roosevelt at least, he brought about this change while expressing his devotion to the principles of the American founding. Roosevelt rightly recognized this as the key to responsible democratic leadership. Responsible democratic leadership, he further believed, was executive leadership because executive power was the only true "steward of the public welfare." Only the executive can put the nation's needs before the lesser interests of the country. Equally important, the executive provides the only antidote to the "impotence which springs from overdivision of governmental power."[11]

This is one of the topics Roosevelt addressed in his autobiography. In his chapter on "The Presidency," he described two conflicting theories on presidential representation and leadership. The first, which he labeled the Lincoln-Jackson school, believed the president is "bound to serve the people affirmatively in cases where the Constitution does not explicitly forbid him to render the service." The second, which he argued was followed with equal sincerity, was the Buchanan-Taft school. This school of thought took a "narrowly legalistic view" of presidential power because it considered the president to be "the servant of the Congress rather than the people." As such, the president could do nothing "no matter how necessary it be to act, unless the Constitution explicitly commands the action."[12]

Roosevelt had absolutely no use for the Buchanan-Taft school of executive submission. The Lincoln-Jackson school was the only one that fit his notion of executive and constitutional responsibility. An inactive president was one who turned the country over to Congress and the regional and special interests it represents. The president is the only voice of the true American majority; democracy requires that that voice not be silenced. So, according to Roosevelt, democracy can exist only where there is a strong and active executive.

An active executive must be knowledgeable as well. Another aspect of responsible leadership is recognizing what is possible given the circumstances that surround the political moment. Roosevelt captured the sense of this when he observed:

> The greatness of our nation in the past has rested upon the fact that the people had power, and that they used it aright for great and worthy ends. Washington and Lincoln, *each in the degree that his generation rendered possible*, trusted to and believed in the people, steadfastly refused to represent anything save what was highest and best in the people, and by appealing to this highest and best brought it out and made it prominent. (emphasis added)[13]

A good leader has faith in the people but only to the degree that his generation renders it possible. Democratic leadership requires striving for what is "highest and best in the people" but it also requires that the leader understand the limits of the people. Roosevelt was keenly aware of the demands both George Washington and Lincoln made on the people. Their success was as much a function of their having realistic expectations as it was of their having a clear political vision.

Roosevelt further realized that Washington and Lincoln had two distinct tasks to perform during their period of political leadership: "Each called upon his countrymen to lay down their lives for an ideal, and then called upon the survivors to perform the even harder task of leading their lives in such shape as to realize the ideal for which the dead men had died."[14] Roosevelt, unfortunately, had only the harder task before him. And the difficulty of that task was made even greater because Roosevelt could not appeal to the blood of a revolution or civil war when expressing the need for a new level of democratic citizenship. Yet Roosevelt understood the power of such appeals and made the necessary rhetorical compensations. For him, the progressive cause was a vital part of the American Revolution and the Civil War because it was part of that ongoing battle for "the good of mankind."

He made the progressive cause one that transcended all individual, geographical, and historical boundaries. Echoing the universal appeal of the Declaration of Independence he argued: "Our cause is the cause of justice for all in the interest of all. Our cause is but a phase of the larger struggle." His full description of this "larger struggle" illustrates how words can be used to argue one point while they vividly demonstrate the contrary. In this case, Roosevelt claimed that neither he nor any other person is important when compared to the larger cause, yet the power of his own words shows why this is not true.

> What happens to me is not of the slightest consequence; I am to be used, as in a doubtful battle any man is used, to his hurt or not, so long as he is useful, and is then cast aside or left to die. I wish you to feel this. I mean it; and I shall need no sympathy when you are through with me, for this fight is far too great to permit us to concern ourselves about any one man's welfare. If we are true to ourselves by putting far above our own interest the triumph of the high cause for which we battle, we shall not lose. It would be far better to fail honorably for the cause we champion than it would be to win by foul methods the foul victory for which our opponents hope. But the victory shall be ours, and it shall be won as we have already won so many victories, by clean and honest fighting for the loftiest of causes. We fight in honorable fashion for the good of mankind; fearless of the future; unheeding of our individual fates; with unflinching hearts and undimmed eyes; we stand at Armageddon, and we battle for the Lord.[15]

Few statements better depict the kind of vision a true statesman must bring to a cause. It is the kind of vision and the kind of rhetoric that give a cause its transcendent quality.

Roosevelt correctly maintained that the task of progressive leadership was no different from the task that had faced previous American leaders.

What was different was the degree to which the progressive generation rendered this task possible. The constant in American leadership is the task of appealing to what is "highest and best in the people" in the hope of making that a "prominent" characteristic of the people. Responsible leadership cannot appeal to just any popular sentiments, only the highest and best. Discerning what is highest and best in the citizens at any given time is the first task of a true leader—the uncommon democratic citizen. For this is the variable that changes from one generation to another.

This aspect of Roosevelt's teachings on leadership was surprisingly close to that expressed by the founders and Lincoln. Roosevelt's concern for and interest in the role human nature must play in understanding politics was what revealed this similarity. He never lost sight of one of the first responsibilities of government, a responsibility expressed most ably by Madison in *Federalist* 51: "You must first enable the government to control the governed." The necessity for this control, even in a democratic society—or especially in a democratic society—was divulged by Roosevelt when he admitted that "the chief dangers to each man dwell within that man's own heart and brain; and what is true of each of us individually is true of all of us in a mass." [16]

Despite the dangers that "dwell within," Roosevelt remained optimistic about Americans in general. This optimism formed the foundation of his most fundamental political beliefs. His views on political parties and the Constitution were a result of this optimism. On the Constitution, this attitude led him to agree with Croly on the need to make the amending process simpler and more popular. But, even while agreeing with Croly, Roosevelt was less extreme and hostile toward the Constitution in particular and laws in general.

One of Roosevelt's most detailed discussions on the nature and purpose of constitutions occurred when he addressed the Ohio Constitutional Convention on February 21, 1912. [17] This address was also one of his most detailed and comprehensive statements on the overall purpose of government and the role progressive reforms must perform within that context. Early in this speech, Roosevelt professed to be an emphatic "believer in constitutionalism." He followed this profession with some insightful comments on why constitutions exist. He first observed: "All constitutions, those of the States no less than that of the nation, are designed, and must be interpreted and administered so as to fit human rights." He expanded on this point when he further stated: "The object of every American constitution worth calling such must be what it is set forth to be in the preamble of the National Constitution, 'to establish justice,' that is, to secure justice as between man and man by means of genuine popular self-

government.'' The qualifier ''worth calling such'' is central to his definition of a constitution. This is also what allowed Roosevelt to defend constitutions as progressive instruments.

To illustrate his point, Roosevelt provided a brief comparison between
the constitutionalism of Lincoln and the constitutionalism of James Buchanan. Not surprisingly, Lincoln's constitutionalism advanced human
rights and justice while Buchanan's ''attempted the reverse.'' Roosevelt
argued that Buchanan's constitutionalism ''attempted to fit human rights
to, and limit them by, the Constitution''; such misuse ''upheld the Constitution as an instrument for the protection of privilege and of vested
wrong.'' False constitutionalism of this kind is unworthy of the name.
Worse than this, it is generally this kind of constitutionalism that is used
to make a mockery of popular rule. Croly, we should remember, saw all
constitutionalism as this type. Roosevelt's broader understanding of constitutionalism rendered it more useful to his cause. He realized that constitutions are written in ''general language'' so they could be tailored to
''fit changing conditions as they occur.''[18] So it was not constitutions that
reinforced the reactionary elements in America during his day, it was the
judges who interpreted the constitutions.

The solution to the problem of constitutional interpretation was simple
according to Roosevelt: let the people ''after due deliberation and discussion'' settle all matters of constitutional construction ''finally and without
appeal.'' But he also felt that judges needed to be made more responsive
to the people in general. Curiously, he cited John Marshall as one of the
three greatest political figures in our national history. He argued that
''under some circumstances'' the office of chief justice was as important
to the nation as was the office of president. In contrast to the founders'
view, Roosevelt considered the chief justice of the United States to be
''like the President, the representative of all the people.''[19] All judges, he
continued, must act as ''a representative of the permanent popular will.''
His understanding of what constituted the ''permanent popular will'' was
expressed on numerous occasions. One of those occasions was a banquet
of the Iroquois Club of Chicago in 1905, where he affirmed that ''all good
Americans are one'' in their ''firm determination that this country shall
remain in the future as it has been in the past, a country of liberty and
justice expressed through the forms of law.''[20]

If judges were to represent the people in their administration of the law,
they needed to recognize the proper role laws must perform within that
society. For Roosevelt, this required following the interpretive approach
set by sociological interpretation.[21] One of the judicial scholars he liked
quoting was Roscoe Pound who, arguing the case for sociological jurispru-

dence against mechanical jurisprudence, asserted: "Law is a means, not an end. We must not make the mistake in American legal education of creating a permanent gulf between legal thought and popular thought." It was such gulfs that permitted the law to serve special interests and privilege first and the bulk of American citizens second. The relationship of the courts to the law and the law to society at large is further illustrated in a quote Roosevelt extracted from *The Churchman*:

> "If the Constitution does not live and expand with the life of the Nation, it becomes a mere letter and fetter which will either strangle the life or have to be broken by it. And to make the Supreme Court a mere guard over the letter without jurisdiction over the spirit and life is to make it an instrument of slow death."[22]

This understanding of the law and of judicial interpretation was very much a product of the progressive movement. This has proved to be one of the most lasting and effective contributions Progressives made to American political thought.

The next question to be raised is: How did political parties fit into Roosevelt's political equation? On one level, this question can be answered by his actions. He was always an active member of a political party; it was not always the same political party, but he never campaigned as an independent. For this reason it seems safe to conclude that he never gave up on political parties as an important instrument of American politics.

Roosevelt did not discuss political parties in any great detail. His fragmented comments on parties and the party system were generally made in passing while he discussed some other topic. However, when these comments are viewed in the light of his actions, a reasonably consistent pattern emerges. Every utterance and action by Roosevelt indicated that he did not accept the view expressed by Croly and others that parties had outlived their usefulness. He accepted parties as an important, if not necessary, political instrument throughout his life.

Roosevelt's continued support of the American party system put him at odds with a number of his Progressive allies. Croly, for instance, never would have argued as Roosevelt did in 1905: "Our country is governed, and under existing circumstances can only be governed, under the party system."[23] In 1912 he echoed this sentiment when he noted: "The system of party government is not written in our constitution, but it is none the less a vital and essential part of our form of government."[24] No matter how frustrated he became with the existing parties, he never rejected the party system as a central element of American politics.

When Roosevelt abandoned the Republican party to join the Progressive party, he acknowledged that while particular parties may come and go, the party system was here to stay. And stay it should, because "the proper aim of the party system is after all simply to subserve the public good." He was able to maintain his commitment to political parties, in part, because he kept them in perspective. "It is alright and inevitable that we should divide on party lines," he argued, "but woe to us if we are not Americans first, and party men second."[25] This perspective made it easier for him to keep the relationship of parties to the Constitution and the American people clearly in focus. By not exaggerating their importance, he did not have to forsake them when times got rough.

After the 1912 campaign Roosevelt made some additional observations that shed further light on his understanding of the nature and role parties perform within our system. Reflecting on the failure of the Progressive party in 1912 he observed: "Our platform of 1912 was rather too advanced for the average man. Our typical leadership was also a little advanced along the lines of morality and loftiness of aim for the average man to follow." After acknowledging these shortcomings he noted a key obstacle to any future hope for success. "Finally, we have to deal with certain political habits that have become very deep-rooted in our people. The average man is a Democrat or a Republican and he is this as a matter of faith, not as a matter of morals."[26] So while these people may bolt their traditional party to punish it, once they have demonstrated their willingness to vote for an opposition party, they return to their original party and their old political habits.

The sober, reflective Roosevelt was still wrestling with the decision he made in 1912. He had expected a party realignment after the 1896 election. He expected that realignment to do for the Progressive party in 1912 what the realignment of the mid-nineteenth century had done for the Republican party. This was a common theme in his speeches once he joined the Progressive party, but he never developed that theme more openly or systematically than he did in his speech at the Lincoln Day banquet in 1913. Yet his efforts to make the Progressive party the heir to the Republican party failed.

The Progressive party's failure in 1912 was due to more than just the habits cited above. Its failure was due to its attracting "great multitudes of cranks" as well. Most of these he considered to be emotionalists who were destructive of the cause. He ended his reflections on the Progressive party's dilemma with the following:

> Then, there is the perfectly proper feeling that there is only room for two parties, the party in power and the opposition. The immediately effective

vote is always for one of these two parties. We were in the position of the
Free Soil party, not of the early Republican party. Finally, in this election
the fundamental question that interested the average man was the purely economic question of how he could best shape conditions so that he could earn
his own living. The workingman was not interested in social and industrial
justice.[27]

This comment is important because it provides a glimpse at his understanding of why our party system has remained a two-party system. It is
also important because despite his disappointment in the "average man's"
disinterest in "social and industrial justice" Roosevelt maintained his
great faith in the average American.

In the final analysis, Roosevelt's unswerving faith in the character of
the average American was what set him apart from the Progressives observed in the previous chapter. Roosevelt and his Progressive colleagues
called for similar reforms and a good portion of their rhetoric was similar
as well, yet Roosevelt was far more consistent than the academic progressive of the preceding chapter. His greater consistency appeared to be a
direct result of his efforts to base his political theory on an understanding
of human nature instead of some vaguely stated historical determinism.

The best way to illustrate this difference is by returning to the writings
of Croly and Duncan-Clark. Nothing reveals the genuine limitations to
their claims better than their own words. In the preceding chapter I cited
Duncan-Clark's statement about the wide diffusion of knowledge and how
this altered the role of leadership in American politics. Progressives argued that Americans had become more enlightened but, by their own
omission, there were limits to the diffusion of knowledge—limits that colleges, magazines, and fast mail apparently could not overcome:

> The average man and woman, busy with the multitudinous affairs of life, has
> not the time for the wide study necessary to cover the far range of this partic-
> ular phase of Progressive interest and propaganda. It is the purpose of the
> following chapters to condense the abundant material available to those of
> larger leisure, and to bring within brief compass and easy reach the substance
> of much research on the part of diligent students and advanced thinkers in
> order that those with limited time and opportunity may be in possession of
> the important facts and main arguments supporting the constructive human
> welfare programme of the Progressive movement.[28]

Apparently there are limits to what the "raised" average of intelligence
can comprehend. He also admitted, whether he realized it or not, that there
is information that is not readily available through magazines and fast
mail. Duncan-Clark was not the only progressive writer to admit these
limitations. Croly made a similar, if not more frightening, admission in

The Promise of American Life. In one of his more candid discussions on leadership, Croly concluded: "The ultimate power to command must rest with the authority which, if necessary, can force people to obey; and any plan of association which seeks to ignore the part which physical force plays in life is necessarily incomplete."[29] So much for the educated masses leading the charge: on the surface, progressivism rarely talked about the need to "force the people to obey."

But this was not Croly's last word on the issue. A page later, he praised democracy by arguing that it was the "best machinery as yet developed for raising the level of human association." What made it the best, at least temporarily, was that "it really teaches men how they must feel, what they must think, and what they must do, in order that they may live together amicably and profitably."[30] If they were slow learners, we know from his earlier statement that physical force might be used to achieve their compliance. Roosevelt claimed that the "bull-dozer" was a tool of the party machines; it appears to have been a tool as well of those "advanced thinkers" who were advocating greater democracy. Consent took on new meaning for Croly and Duncan-Clark.

This was one area where the academic progressives and the political progressives were not in perfect alignment. Roosevelt seemed to be more in agreement with our constitutional founders on this issue than was either Croly or Duncan-Clark. He once described his style of leadership in this way:

> People always use to say of me that I was an astonishingly good politician and divined what the people were going to think. This really was not an accurate way of stating the case. I did not "divine" what the people were going to think; I simply made up my mind what they *ought* to think; and then did my best to get them to think it. Sometimes I failed and then my critics said that "my ambition had overleaped itself." Sometimes I succeeded; and then they said that I was an uncommonly astute creature to have detected what the people were going to think and to pose as their leader in thinking it.[31]

Roosevelt was "uncommonly astute" and his attitude toward leadership relied more on persuasion than coercion. It is in this respect that he followed the tried and true method of the founders who talked about the need to "refine and enlarge the public's view." They were advocating an appeal to human reason, an appeal that would be rooted in open and informed discussion with the American people. Nowhere in the founding documents are there references to the kind of forced compliance suggested by Croly.

We should not be surprised by this revelation. After all, coercion is a fairly common reform tactic. America's more recent party reformers have found it necessary to dictate the terms of openness as well. Nor should it surprise us that Roosevelt did not fall for these heavy-handed tactics.

The majority of Progressive reformers were, no doubt, in Roosevelt's camp on this issue. They accepted the rhetoric of the movement at face value. It was hard to see that, by shifting the focus of American politics from the local party caucus or precinct meeting to some administrative office at the county or national seat of government, they were eroding the very fabric of our constitutional system. The twofold impact of this shift was to make the American political system considerably less democratic and profoundly more unitary. To put it another way, many Progressives seemed to be more comfortable with a popular executive than with a competent executive. Not that one automatically precludes the other, but our history reveals that these two qualities do not necessarily go hand in hand.

Roosevelt's ill-fated presidential campaign of 1912 probably does not deserve all the credit for the changes that have occurred in presidential leadership in this century, and yet his campaign set a standard for presidential leadership that has far surpassed that of any other campaign in this century. When he bolted the Republican party to lead the Progressive charge in 1912, he established, unwittingly no doubt, what would eventually become the norm in presidential leadership—at least in the realm of electoral politics. The Progressive party, in a very important sense, became his own independent campaign organization. When his campaign ended, the people who made up his organization returned to their rightful political homes: the Democratic and Republican parties. The Progressive party was to Roosevelt what the Committee to Re-elect the President was to Richard Nixon. As a Progressive party candidate, Roosevelt was able to campaign as someone who had transcended normal partisan politics.

But more than this, Roosevelt set in motion an attitude about the executive that has dominated the rest of the twentieth century. His approach to presidential campaigning in 1912 made a strong case for a direct link between the president and the people. By so doing, he set in motion a new vision of executive power, one that not only transcended party politics but coalition politics as well.

On the surface this may not appear to be a terribly bold or radical move, for he was far more consistent and honest than some of his Progressive allies. But over the long run, the direct link between the president and the people has had a profound and, no doubt, negative impact on presidential leadership on at least two counts. First, it has made the personality of the presidential candidate more important than the principles of the party. This leads to campaigns that rely more on mobilizing factions than on building coalitions. A power base built on factions can only be maintained by frequent appeals to the people. It is one thing for the citizenry to be the ultimate judge of presidential policies; it is quite another for them to be expected to participate in each step of the development of that policy. The second danger, one that is obviously related to the first, is the shift this brings to presidential-congressional relations—a shift that invites the much maligned "imperial presidency."[32]

Roosevelt, like most of his Progressive colleagues, was so concerned with democratic procedures or means that he seemed to ignore the results these procedures would produce. Party reformers in the late 1960s and 1970s made a similar mistake. Unfortunately, Roosevelt's system for campaigning has been reinforced by media developments (primarily radio and television) and by an increasing desire by presidential candidates to have their own independent campaign organizations.

One of the great strengths of the founders was their careful consideration of both means and ends. The Declaration of Independence and the Preamble to the Constitution establish the highest ends possible for modern government; the rest of our Constitution and our two-party system provide the best means we know for achieving those ends. Reforms may be necessary from time to time, but our most successful reforms have always been those which move us closer to the ideals set forth by our founders, not those which claim to transcend them. Political parties may not have been endorsed by the founders, but they have done an excellent job of preserving those principles and institutions that were. They have also proved to be the best vehicle for presidential leadership: a vehicle that helps the president "refine and enlarge the public's view." The challenge of any republican government is to transform the public's mind "by elevating it from whim to deliberate choice."[33] Contrary to the progressive view, political parties are still the most comprehensive way to accomplish this task.

Roosevelt viewed parties as an important vehicle for change in the American political system. On this score he had a better understanding of their value to American politics than did Croly. In the final analysis, Roosevelt may be judged as a kinder and gentler progressive: rhetorically he appeared less hostile to the Constitution and the two-party system, but practically, he proved to have no better understanding of the ends they were established to achieve.

Chapter Three

Constitutional Government or Party Government?

The extraconstitutional nature of political parties has always posed a problem for students of American politics and history. Politicians, lawyers, academics, even casual observers of our political system, have been forced to devise a variety of intellectual schemes for understanding the awkward relationship that has developed between our political system and our constitutional system. Some scholars have gone so far as to suggest that we have to choose between the two systems because their unhappy union could not long endure. Reformers of every imaginable persuasion have suggested ways to alter our political structure to resolve the conflicts that are inherent in our system of government.

How party reform affects the Constitution is revealed most clearly in the debate over "responsible parties." It is important, however, to keep in mind that not all advocates of responsible government want responsible parties; furthermore, some proponents of responsible parties seem to be unable to develop the necessary formula to create such a system. Even the most ardent defenders of some kind of responsible or parliamentary system find it difficult to tailor the American system so it will conform to a responsible or parliamentary model.

One of the first and probably the best known of the responsible reformers was Woodrow Wilson. His very earliest writings presented his clearest calls for a responsible system of government. He recognized the importance of political parties and, more specifically, the inevitability of parties in republican government. While his commitment to responsible parties was fairly obvious, the means to achieving this end were not very clear. Wilson's commitment was to leadership, first and foremost. Responsible government was a key to good leadership, but responsible government did not necessarily require responsible parties; this leads to some confusion when looking to Wilson for guidance on a responsible party system.

Wilson's dissatisfaction with America's constitutional structure is well documented and fairly consistent. The confusion rests with his apparent uncertainty over the proper solution to these constitutional problems. For Wilson, the evolution of the American political system complicated matters considerably. He seemed to appreciate fully the task that confronted the founders and was largely supportive of their overall scheme of government. However, this did not keep him from arguing that the political system had outgrown some aspects of the founders' plan. In the 1870s and 1880s, he considered the paramount obstacle to responsible leadership to be the founders' excessive devotion to separation of powers.

The solution to this excess, according to Wilson, could be found in a cabinet form of government: "a responsible cabinet constitutes a link between the executive and the legislative departments of the Government which experience declares in the clearest tones to be absolutely necessary in a well-regulated, well-proportioned body politic."[1] The cabinet government he proposed is not a pure party cabinet such as the British possess; herein lies the main confusion over the role of parties within his proposed system.

But before we get too tied down with the details of Wilson's plan for a cabinet government in the United States, it is necessary and instructive to consider his views on political parties in general and their history in the United States in particular. Wilson considered political parties to be an absolute necessity to republican government. According to Wilson: "Representative government is party government; and party government is partisan government. This is the only known means of self-government."[2] But Wilson's commitment was to party government, not necessarily to political parties. This may be cutting a fine line, but it is critical to an understanding of the extent and nature of the reforms being proposed by Wilson.

A leading characteristic of the American party system has always been its decentralized nature—a nature which has made party responsibility elusive in the United States. When the decentralized nature of America's party system is combined with separation of powers, we have a multi-headed creature which is not only geographically divided, but institutionally divided as well. The first task of any statesman interested in leading the nation has been to build coalitions that bridge some of the many divisions within our political system. Coalition building starts with the diverse geographical regions and if one succeeds at that level, the institutional divisions are overcome as well.

Successful party builders in the United States have found it necessary to combine the rhetorical skills of national leaders with the organizational skills of the grass-roots party structure. A strong coordinated effort between the national party leaders and the local organizers has proved very effective at mobilizing public opinion in American politics. Such coordination calls for considerable ability on the part of national leaders because the diverse geographical makeup of the United States mandates that any broad appeal be rooted in sound political principle. Policy appeals cannot unite the diverse segments of our extended republic.

Historically, the kinds of principles that have provided the basis for party appeals were those that guided the founding generation. James Madison and Martin Van Buren made successful appeals to constitutional principles, and Abraham Lincoln appealed to the principles set forth in the Declaration of Independence. Although these principles were linked to some specific policies or issues, their broad appeal was due to their transcendent quality. It was the link to some understanding of overriding principle that gave the issues their mass appeal. Wilson seemed to recognize this fact when he observed:

> It is an interesting but apparently unobserved fact of American history that almost all the greatest statesmen of the Union have been constitutional lawyers rather than masters of administrative policy. The great battles of our politics have been fought around the Constitution, and the exposition of that splendid instrument has furnished almost every bone of contention. . . . Constitutional issues have been the tides, matters of administrative policy only the eddies. Even to the present day parties claim to take character from views of the Constitution which have been handed down from party to party from the earliest hours of the Union.[3]

At the heart of all these constitutional issues, according to Wilson, was the question of the proper construction of the Constitution: the national supremacists taking one side and the states-rights advocates taking the other.[4]

Wilson further believed that the constitutional focus of partisan battles was no longer possible in the post-Civil War era because "The construction of the Constitution is settled now, settled once and for all by the supreme arbitrament of war. Sections no longer stand at deadly variance."[5] With the demise of the one constitutional issue that created political parties Wilson believed that parties would cease to exist. The only thing left for parties to fight over was patronage and that simply was not an adequate base for maintaining a real party system.

The battle over spoils created "unnatural and unholy coalitions" that could be broken up only by switching government jobs over to a civil service system. But such a change would require leadership and that was hard to develop in the absence of lofty constitutional issues. Without great constitutional issues to attract them, statesmen had become scarce in America. This situation led Wilson to the following conclusion: "Eight words contain the sum of the present degradation of our political parties: No leaders, no principles; no principles, no parties. Congressional leadership is divided infinitesimally; and with divided leadership there can be no great party units."[6]

The new challenge for American politics in general and party politics in particular was leadership. According to Wilson, the British model for governing presented the best and purest model for leadership available:

> England has thus adopted the simplest and most straight-forward method of party government. The chiefs of the party which has secured the largest representation in the Commons are entrusted with the administration of the government and with the direction of legislation. That party majority would in any case control the policy of the government, and the most honest way for it to rule is that which it has chosen, of putting itself under the leadership of those men of its own ranks who have proved their ability to lead, and entrusting to those leaders the responsible duties of rule.[7]

Such responsible leadership necessitates a cabinet form of government which Wilson described as the "greatest of all popular governments."[8]

For Wilson, a cabinet government would solve a variety of problems in the American political system, all of which contributed to our lack of political leadership. The first of these problems was the increasing fragmentation of Congress, due primarily to the increasing importance of the standing committees. The importance of standing committees led Wilson to conclude that the United States was in fact a "Committee Government." The second problem that would be addressed by a cabinet government was the weakened executive. The Constitution created a weak executive, but time, according to Wilson, had further eroded executive authority. The third problem to be solved by a cabinet government was the weakening of America's political parties. This last point is, no doubt, of greatest interest to this study, but Wilson's assessment of the problem and his proposed solution require a comprehensive examination. After all, political parties are extraconstitutional institutions whose very purpose is to influence, if not control, the seats of constitutional power.

The problems caused by a fragmented legislature were the gravest in Wilson's eyes because "the legislature has become the imperial power of State, as it must of necessity become under every representative system."[9] Wilson had no problem accepting the "necessity" of an imperial Congress; the problem he perceived was with "a legislature which is practically irresponsible for its acts."[10] Since all legislation is referred to standing committees, Congress, especially the House of Representatives, "very seldom takes any direct action upon any measures introduced by individual members; its votes and discussions are almost entirely confined to committee reports and committee dictation. The whole attitude of business depends upon forty-seven Standing Committees."[11] The real discussions of the nation's business take place within committees, "whose proceedings must from their very nature be secret," and it is this secrecy that is both "dangerous and unwholesome."

Wilson accepted legislative dominion in government because, as he stated in "Cabinet Government": "At its highest development, *representative* government is that form which best enables a free people to govern themselves. The main object of a representative assembly, therefore, should be the discussion of public business."[12] But this is not the case in the Congress. In one of his most complete and damning assaults on committee government, Wilson concluded:

> Curtailment and discouragement of debate, then, seem to be—nay, do not seem to be, but *are*—the vices of committee government which make its condemnation certain. It is a system which can stand neither the test of philosophy nor the test of common-sense. . . . The lack of openness alone is sufficient to damn it. . . . For it should be noted what a host of ugly mischiefs are covered by this cloak of privacy, and that no facile expedition of business can compensate for the license of deceit it gives.[13]

He went on to predict that the committee system of government would not survive and that America would be forced to give way to "the prevailing legislative practice of the world"—cabinet government.

Secrecy was not, however, the only problem posed by committee government. Another problem created by irresponsible committees was that there "is no one in Congress to speak for the nation." Despite the great powers held by the Speaker of the House (these were considerable back in the late 1800s), his main control rested in his power over the standing committees, but once the membership and chairmanship of these committees were set, each functioned as a separate fiefdom, rendering Congress "a conglomeration of inharmonious elements." Congress was guided by a series of local interests, each possessing control over some particular committee which rendered legislation "at best only a limping compromise between the conflicting interests of the innumerable localities represented." The result of this system was a Congress with "no guiding or harmonizing power."[14]

Attracting leaders to such a divided system is an additional shortcoming. Committee government makes all the "prizes of leadership small" and, therefore, "unattractive to minds of the highest order." Young Wilson considered this a major flaw in the political system because "the only real leadership in governmental affairs must be legislative leadership" in a representative democracy.[15]

The contrast between this early Wilson and the later or Progressive Wilson is most acute when we consider the executive branch. The Progressive literature cited in earlier chapters envisioned a political system built around the executive. Clearly, Wilson switched to this position by 1908 when he published *Constitutional Government*. This later work condemned the founders for following the "Whig theory of political dynamics."[16] Here, Wilson advocated viewing constitutions from a Darwinian perspective instead of a Newtonian perspective, but the Wilson we are examining now is the congressional Wilson, the academic Wilson, the Wilson of the nineteenth century.

Wilson regretted that our constitutional founders seemed to regard the "British Cabinet as an institution peculiar to monarchical government."[17] This, he argued, was an unfortunate result of historical timing, for later developments revealed cabinet government to be "a safe and effective instrument of popular party government." Since this was not apparent in 1789, our constitutional founders agonized over the proper role and function of the executive. Only one participant at the 1789 convention appeared to have the foresight to recognize the virtues of a cabinet system, according to Wilson. Roger Sherman recognized the executive's subordination to the legislature:

> the executive magistracy as nothing more than an institution for carrying the will of the legislature into effect; that the person or persons who should constitute the executive ought to be appointed by and accountable to, the legislature only, which was the depository of the supreme will of society.[18]

Wilson not only considered legislative selection of the executive to be an attractive option, he was also attracted to the proposal for a multiple executive. Both of these alternatives would have pointed in the direction of a cabinet government. Wilson regretted that other men at the convention were unconvinced by Sherman's views on the executive. His position on the executive was especially insightful, in Wilson's eyes, given the way the office had developed.

Wilson correctly recognized that the executive branch of our government was growing more complex, a complexity that he believed had altered the very nature of the executive. He summarized the change in the following manner:

But when now-a-days we speak of "the Executive" we generally mean not only this single chief magistrate, not the President alone, though his is the head and front of the executive organization, but the heads of the several Departments as well. Executive duties are now exceedingly multifarious, and cannot all, of course, be performed even under his immediate supervision.[19]

He also noted that the Constitution speaks only of the president when it discusses the executive. This, according to Wilson, was a major difference between the constitutional executive and the functioning executive. What had remained constant was the subordination of the executive to the supreme will of the legislature.

Wilson was especially concerned about the changing role of cabinet members within the executive. The role the first cabinet performed in the political system was quite distinct: "They were always recognized units in the system, never mere ciphers to the Presidential figure which led them. Their wills counted as independent wills."[20] Wilson noted that this change was due in large part to the development of political parties. Since those early years the role and function of the cabinet have been left to the whims of the president, so the real nature of the executive may alter with each election. The varying backgrounds and training of each cabinet member influence the executive branch almost as much as do the talents and temperament of the president. Wilson was very uncomfortable with the uncertainty of the cabinet's position within the government.

Wilson's disdain for the notion of a citizen politician had implications across the political system but was especially acute in the executive arena. "Efficiency is the only just foundation for confidence in a public officer," he argued, "and short terms which cut off the efficient as surely and inexorably as the inefficient are quite as repugnant to republican as to monarchical rules of wisdom." There were a number of causes for this inefficiency. One of the most obvious was the set term of office: "A President," he argued, "is dismissed almost as soon as he learned the duties of office."[21] Wilson's most extreme recommendation to address this problem was to have presidents appointed for life or "during good behavior."[22] On other occasions he recommended extending the term of office without specifying the desirable length. This concern was closely tied to his desire for a cabinet system with elections linked to confidence votes that would dissolve at least the House of Representatives.[23]

The nature of the executive is greatly influenced by the method of selection. As might be expected, Wilson had strong opinions on this topic as well. Many aspects of the selection system dissatisfied him but, basically, he resented the lack of congressional involvement in the process. Let us not forget that his primary, if not his sole, purpose for creating a cabinet system was to tie the executive and legislative branches closer together. At one time political parties facilitated this all-important link, but they do so no more. Wilson argued that parties had changed the very nature of the electoral process. Moreover, this was not limited to the nomination process. For him, the electors had become "merely a registering machine,—a sort of bell-punch to the hand of his party convention."[24]

As might be expected, this discussion leads directly to the role and function of political parties. Herein lies the heart and soul of Wilson's concern and this is what makes him an important figure in this study. Many factors contributed to the weakening of political parties but those associated with the executive will be considered first.

For Wilson, the presidential electors had passed through a series of distinct stages. At first the electors were to vote their conscience, "for the Constitution bade them to vote as deemed best." This period lasted for only the first two presidential contests. By the third presidential election the choice became much harder, and party managers were able to secure electors who were committed to a particular candidate before they were chosen. This quickly led to the period of congressional oversight of the electoral process: "From 1800 to 1824 there was an unbroken succession of caucuses of the Republican members of Congress to direct the action of the party electors." Wilson considered this to be a very "logical mode of party government" and regretted that it had not been a more open system.[25] With the demise of the congressional caucuses the path was clear for the development of national conventions, the first of which appeared in 1832.

Wilson had no difficulty accepting electors who were instruments of congressional caucuses, but nominating conventions were a different matter altogether, even though both systems selected candidates for the presidency for reasons other than legislative ability. This was a weakness in both systems according to Wilson, because he considered that the president's greatest powers were legislative.[26] Even members of Congress who had received their party's nomination were chosen because of other abilities they possessed. "Andrew Jackson had been a member of Congress, but he was chosen President because he had won the battle of New Orleans and had driven the Indians from Florida." America's premier legislators (he cited Daniel Webster and Henry Clay) seemed incapable of making it to the White House. In later years, Wilson himself would occupy the presidency without ever serving in Congress.

This shortcoming was not a weakness of parties per se, only a weakness of American parties. I have already cited Wilson's commitment to political parties as an indispensable component of republican government. Wilson felt that the mixture of poor leadership and spoils had produced considerable decay in America's party system:

> The danger consists not in the existence of parties, but in the existence of corrupt parties; and the salvation of the government depends, not upon the abolition of parties, but upon their proper control. If our parties were so open in their operations that the nation could see what they do and why they do it, their purity would be ensured, because their responsibility would be complete.[27]

Party corruption was the direct result of irresponsibility, and irresponsibility was a direct result of diffused leadership. Separation of powers, federalism, and committee government provided too many focal points for leadership. Leadership was possible in America but only under the most extreme circumstances. "Crises give birth and a new growth to statesmanship because they are peculiarly periods of action, in which talents find the widest and the freest scope." Wilson further acknowledged that crisis provides "opportunity for transcendent influence, therefore, which calls into active public life a nation's greater minds,—minds which might otherwise remain absorbed in the smaller affairs of private life."[28]

This is certainly one of the many lessons of history. But Wilson believed that responsible leadership can and will provide many more opportunities for leadership; opportunities that will cultivate and create a constant need for leadership. This, he argued, is the "cardinal feature of Cabinet government." But, it must be noted, this is not the same kind of leadership Madison described in *Federalist* 51 or that Lincoln discussed in his speech to the Young Men's Lyceum in 1838. Wilson was describing leaders who demonstrated "administrative talent" or agility "upon the floor of Congress."[29] These are, indeed, no mean skills, but they do not require the towering intellect or creative genius of a Jefferson, a Lincoln, or even a Roosevelt.

Wilson's scheme would create an institutional means for leadership that was not and is not available to party leaders under our current system of government. This would make leadership easier to acquire, but that would be due, in part, to his lowering the skills necessary to assume leadership. Under our decentralized system, as was noted earlier, it takes someone with rare statesmanlike qualities to unify the nation and the different institutions that govern our nation. But this is by design.

At least one of the shortcomings of America's party system was historical in nature. With the demise of constitutional issues, the parties' ability to appeal to principles died as well. In the absence of principles, parties have no common rallying point:

They are not homogeneous but conglomerate—the one representing all who
are hoping for office, the other made up of every faction that is opposed to
the party which is in power. The Republicans are the "ins," the Democrats
the "outs"—and that is the long and the short of it. Our political orators,
therefore, have no themes. . . . They cannot establish personal leadership for
themselves under our system, which *individualizes* and does not combine.[30]

Wilson rightfully linked leadership with oratory and recognized that
oratory cannot be built around thin air or administrative efficiency. The
Civil War settled the last issue that could attract statesmen to American
politics and our constitutional system of checks and balances would keep
them away.

When America had fundamental issues to divide the nation, the inconvenience of separation of powers was overcome, but can be no more. In
the absence of lofty principles only power can attract great people to government. Yet it was (and is) a central feature of the American constitutional
system to deny real power to any and everyone. This was the train of
thought that led Wilson to conclude that America had evolved beyond the
old constitutional system that had been designed by the founders. Political
parties were central to Wilson's scheme because they could cure our political ailment, but not as they existed in the late 1800s. Parties were able to
unite the separate branches of government when the stakes were high, but
the stakes no longer were high and, according to Wilson's reasoning, never
would be again.

Wilson's opinion can be summarized in the following manner. Once the
key constitutional issue was settled, the Constitution needed to be
changed; it was only the battles over proper construction of the document
that allowed us to overcome the flaws within the document.

Wilson's assault on the Constitution in the name of party government
was the first major attack on the work of the founders since John C. Calhoun's in the 1830s. Interestingly, Calhoun felt consensus was too easily
established under our constitutional system whereas Wilson argued the
contrary. In *Congressional Government*, Wilson acknowledged the nov-
elty of his opposition to the Constitution.

We are the first Americans to hear our own countrymen ask whether the
Constitution is still adapted to serve the purposes for which it was intended;
the first to entertain any serious doubts about the superiority of our own
institutions as compared with the systems of Europe; the first to think of
remodeling the administrative machinery of the federal government, and of
forcing new forms of responsibility upon Congress.[31]

Wilson later argued:

> The noble charter of fundamental law given us by the Convention of 1787 is still our Constitution; but it is now our *form of government* rather in name than in reality, the form of the Constitution being one of nicely adjusted, ideal balances, whilst the actual form of our present government is simply a scheme of congressional supremacy.[32]

A responsible party system of government would allow us not only to solve the leadership problem that confronted our nation but would also permit us to bring the Constitution in line with political realities.

Numerous changes in our constitutional system would be needed. The most important of these changes would be to add four words to Article I, Section 6, Clause 2. This clause prohibits members of Congress from holding "any civil office under the authority of the United States" and further states that "no person holding any office under the United States, shall be a member of either house during his continuance in office." Obviously this clause is an important, if not the most important, contributor to separation of powers. Wilson's suggested change would have read "and no person holding any *other than a Cabinet* office under the United States shall be a member of either house during his continuance in office." He correctly acknowledged that this change "will have removed the chief constitutional obstacle to the erection of Cabinet government in this country."[33]

Wilson admitted that while this was the crucial amendment, additional amendments would be needed. The most notable of these would be changing the terms of office for the president and members of the House of Representatives. In exchange for longer terms of office Wilson would add "the principle of ministerial responsibility,—that is, the resignation of the Cabinet upon the defeat of any important part of their plans." This is a key feature of responsible government.[34] So at a minimum we would need at least four amendments to the Constitution: one abolishing separation of powers, one to extend the president's term in office, one to extend the term of House members, and one that would permit the dissolving of the House after a no-confidence vote.

At one point Wilson argued that the extension of terms of office would not alter any *principle*, admitting that letting members of Congress hold cabinet positions was "the only change of principle called for."[35] Wilson certainly realized that "the only change of principle" he was advocating constituted the central principle of our constitutional system. The constitutional founders considered nothing more important to our system of government than the principle of separation of powers. Madison highlighted the importance of this principle when he argued in *Federalist* 47: "The accumulation of all powers legislative, executive and judicial in the same hands, whether of one, a few or many, and whether hereditary, self appointed, or elective, may justly be pronounced the very definition of tyranny."

Yet this is the very accumulation that Wilson was advocating when he called for the abolition of separation of powers by the one amendment specifically proposed above. While Wilson justified this accumulation of power, in part, by claiming that it is the reality of our evolved political situation, he also claimed that the founders erred when they created this separation: "A complete separation of the executive and legislative is not in accord with the true spirit of those essentially English institutions of which our Government is a characteristic offshoot."[36] Wilson believed that our historical roots were more important than our theoretical roots; our link to the British empire was more important than our link to our own founders.

The British influence in Wilson's early works is quite apparent. Walter Lippmann claimed that Wilson believed that the "history of the English people is also the history of the American people."[37] There is, of course, a good deal of truth to this belief and yet it does not make British history— after 1776—more important to American political institutions than America's own political history—after 1776. Regardless of Wilson's opinions, there is no justification for considering Walter Bagehot a more authoritative source for American constitutionalism than Publius. Wilson's admiration for Bagehot is clearly discernible in most, if not all, of his early political writings and Bagehot's criticism of the American system of government obviously becomes Wilson's. But that does not justify his trying to discredit *The Federalist* as "an authoritative constitutional manual."

Wilson's political histories were more prescriptive than descriptive. He simply did not agree with the theoretical assumptions of the founding generation, at least not with those which ultimately prevailed. In this respect, the responsible Wilson and the progressive Wilson were one; neither Wilson found the "auxiliary precautions" that were (and are) the cornerstone of our constitutional system necessary or desirable. Wilson was a consistent majoritarian, given his understanding of democratic majoritarianism.[38] While Wilson may not have been terribly original in his political writings he did establish a precedent that would prove to be a major undercurrent in the American political system for the next century. That undercurrent was his proposal that party government become the alternative to the constitutional government devised and established by the founders.

Wilson's pioneering efforts on behalf of political parties must be recognized for what they were: not a call for reform of the American party system but a call for radical restructuring of the entire American political landscape. Wilson's proposals were the most radical and politically uprooting proposals set forth by any responsible American since the actions of the Continental Congress on July 2, 1776. Clearly, what he was advocating was more radical than had been the actions taken by our constitutional founders in 1787. For as great as the changes were between the Articles of Confederation and the Constitution, each document accepted the need for institutional restraints on the will of the majority.

Wilson's call for a responsible government was motivated by a desire to dismantle those institutional restraints. He genuinely believed that the old constitutional system of institutional checks not only thwarted the will of the majority but was also the chief cause of administrative inefficiency. As was noted above, there was no reason to be suspicious of administrative efficiency now that the one constitutional issue that had divided the country was settled. But it was more than the settled Constitution that made efficient government desirable to Wilson. We cannot forget his devotion to leadership, a devotion so strong that he could argue: "The most despotic of Governments under the control of wise statesmen is preferable to the freest ruled by demagogues."[39] Such Platonic utterances are not the normal forensic tools of democrats—ancient or modern.

This apparent contradiction is just that in Wilson's political universe. When party government replaces constitutional government, the masses will assess the conflicting parties on their ability to administer. In the absence of constitutional conflict, this is all that will distinguish one party from the other.[40] Wilson seemed to believe that wise statesmen will certainly prove to be better administrators than either unwise statesmen or demagogues and, therefore, will continue to be reelected until someone wiser comes along. This is perfectly consistent with Wilson's view of democracy; responsible parties not only facilitate this function but are an essential ingredient in his political scheme.

Wilson's desire to have party government replace constitutional government has met with little political success but it has been a smashing success in academic circles. The twentieth century has been punctuated with calls for a responsible party system. The irony of this is that Wilson proposed responsible parties as a practical solution to the theoretically deficient system of the founders. Today, Wilson's responsible party system remains one of the leading theoretical alternatives to our constitutional system.

It must be noted that, in the final analysis, Wilson was as much responsible for the failure of party government as anyone. Reformers at the turn of the century dumped the responsible party system for a younger, more attractive companion—the progressive movement. It may be true that the Progressives still desired a responsible system of government, but it was not party-centered. Indeed, the hallmark of the progressive movement was its dependence on the executive: a dependence that Wilson's years in the White House ably represented. The exact timing of Wilson's abandonment of the responsible party movement is unimportant; what is important is that we recognize his shift in loyalty from leadership that was party-centered to leadership that was executive-centered.

There is consistency in Wilson's position, consistency that reveals an important shift in the role and nature of political parties. Wilson's calls for reforms were always designed to strengthen the popular branch of government that he felt was already the stronger. In this respect he made a significant break from the founders of America's party system. Party advocates in the late eighteenth and early nineteenth centuries saw parties as a means to strengthening the weaker member of the political partnership, a move calculated to enhance the integrity of our constitutional system of separation of powers. Wilson's move to strengthen the stronger branch of government was designed to accomplish the exact opposite. This is where Wilson and the rest of the American party reformers parted company from their predecessors—the American party founders.

Chapter Four

Rediscovering Imprudence

The role Woodrow Wilson played in party reform efforts in America shifted when he left the academy and became a political practitioner. As we have seen, the academic Wilson was a responsible party advocate, but the presidential Wilson moved squarely into the progressive camp. He had consistently advocated a stronger role for government, but now he shifted the focal point of that stronger government from the Capitol to the White House. Wilson's journey from one end of Pennsylvania Avenue to the other was an important one in the history of America's party system and thought. He was not alone in his desire to change the center of American government from the Congress to the presidency, but there were a large number of reformers who were uncomfortable with the expanding executive powers. In fact, some reformers felt that the growth in presidential powers made strengthening other components of our national political system more urgent. Not surprisingly, many of these reform advocates continued to look to America's party system as a component central to any reform effort.

The responsible party movement enjoyed a renaissance in the middle of the twentieth century. E. E. Schattschneider was certainly one of the main sources of this revival. His book, *Party Government*, was one of the leading works in resurrecting the push for the movement. In the first chapter of his work, Schattschneider made two basic assumptions about political parties that are of fundamental importance to this inquiry. His first and boldest assertion was: "The parties created democracy, or perhaps more accurately, modern democracy is a by-product of party competition."[1] Whether or not parties created democracy, the relationship between the two is clearly important to any discussion about parties. Schattschneider's second assertion was directed more specifically toward the American political system: "The Constitution made the rise of parties inevitable yet was incompatible with party government."[2] This, too, is a statement deserving the most serious and fundamental consideration. If he was correct about the incompatibility between the Constitution and political parties, it is a miracle that our system has survived for so long given these fundamental inconsistencies. Both statements have elements of truth to them but they are truths that need to be qualified and explained.

Let us begin with Schattschneider's explanation of the problems that confronted party development. He started his examination of political parties in America with a brief and very incomplete look at the arguments James Madison presented in *Federalist* 10. Schattschneider argued that Madison's purpose in this paper was to defend separation of powers and federalism, but, he concluded, Madison outsmarted himself by making such a strong case for federalism that he destroyed the case for separation of powers: "If the multiplicity of interests in a large republic makes tyrannical majorities impossible, the principal theoretical prop of the separation of powers has been demolished."[3] This was wishful thinking on Schattschneider's part, for like his intellectual ally, Wilson, he recognized that separation of powers is *the* obstacle to an American party governmental system.

To develop his case against separation of powers and the Constitution that established that separation, Schattschneider argued that there is an age-old dichotomy between a "lawyers' constitution" and a "politicians' constitution." This dichotomy became the undercurrent for the rest of Schattschneider's argument. The simple response to such a gross oversimplification would be to note that most politicians are lawyers. But Schattschneider deserves a more comprehensive response, and such a response requires that his thesis be explored more fully.

Before we examine the two assertions cited above, we must acknowledge some of the theoretical assumptions that guided Schattschneider's work. First, his theoretical assumptions were historically driven. He argued that not only is there an important distinction between ancient and modern democracies, but that there are some critical changes that have occurred within the American context. I have already noted his belief that modern democracies are a product of political parties. This is the central theme of Schattschneider's work. The second point, which puts parties' transforming qualities in an American context, can be best illustrated by his own words as well:

American parties are important in view of their accomplishments. It can be said justly that they have transformed the American Constitution. They have substantially abolished the electoral college, created a plebiscitary presidency, and contributed powerfully to the extraconstitutional growth of that office. As a result of the efforts of the political parties the President of the

United States today receives a mandate to govern the nation and is responsible for the safety and welfare of the Republic. The parties have greatly simplified the most complex system of government in the world, and we may be certain that the work of reconstruction will continue as long as the party system endures.[4]

His description of what has happened is followed by a prescription of what should happen.

Schattschneider was describing the results of Progressive reforms as much as the results of America's party system. Theodore Roosevelt and Wilson were largely responsible for these changes, especially those related to the presidency. It could be argued that Schattschneider was calling for the solutions advocated by the young Wilson to correct the problems created by the old Wilson. Schattschneider felt that Progressive reforms had given the executive branch too much power. Political parties provide the best, if not the sole, solution to this problem.

But Schattschneider, like the young Wilson, continued to be unhappy with American political parties. Despite the great accomplishments he credited to them in the quotation cited above, he was baffled by the decentralized nature of the American party system. And yet, that decentralized nature was a direct result of federal characteristics established by our constitutional system. What especially frustrated Schattschneider was the same thing that frustrated Wilson, Herbert Croly, and to a lesser extent even Roosevelt: the complexity of the American constitutional system of government.

With all their advanced degrees and learned writing, these reformers never came to an understanding of the political system described so ably by Publius in *The Federalist*. This lack of understanding is revealed in numerous places but rarely is it any clearer than in Schattschneider's critique of the argument presented in *Federalist* 10.

Schattschneider entered his investigation with a blinding prejudice. That prejudice, as noted earlier, was his belief that modern democracies are unthinkable without political parties. This preconceived notion made it hard for him to examine the writings of people who did not share his reverence for political parties. Yet the kinds of formal political parties he equated with modern democracies were unknown to the American founders, largely because they were a result of the founders' work. Political parties may not have been an anticipated result or even a desired result, but they were nevertheless a direct result of the founders' labors.

What made both modern democracies and modern political parties possible was the "new science of politics." Yet Schattschneider could not accept this because it contradicted his case for political parties being the essential ingredient to modern democracies. Still he tried to ignore some of the key characteristics of this new science because parts of it were detrimental to his beloved party system. He rightfully praised the founders for their all-important contribution to the new science: the enlarged sphere. His discussion of *Federalist* 10 was built around his praise of the founders' defense of large republics, but his discussion was flawed because he refused to recognize the necessary and prior discussion that took place in *Federalist* 9.

Schattschneider's refusal to address the new science of politics in its entirety distorted his analysis of the portion he did acknowledge. He failed to realize that this new science—not political parties—was what made modern democracies possible because he refused to consider it as a comprehensive theoretical system. To understand his error fully, we must examine the portion of the new science he ignored.

An essential theoretical perspective links *Federalist* 9 and *Federalist* 10. *Federalist* 9 describes the theoretical foundation of the constitutional system that is developed in all the papers that follow it. It is also Publius's most systematic defense of popular government. Defending popular governments was no easy feat in the eighteenth century. Publius described the challenge when he observed:

> It is impossible to read the history of petty Republics of Greece and Italy, without feeling sensations of horror and disgust at the distractions with which they were continually agitated, and at the rapid succession of revolutions, by which they were kept in a state of perpetual vibration, between the extremes of tyranny and anarchy.

Publius continued this observation by stating that if republican governments promised no cure for these problems, "the enlightened friends of liberty would have been obliged to abandon the cause of this species of government as indefensible." But, fortunately, Publius recognized that there had been theoretical breakthroughs to solve these historical problems:

> The science of politics, . . . like most other sciences has received great improvements. The efficiency of various principles is now well understood, which were either not known at all, or imperfectly known to the ancients. The regular distribution of power into distinct departments—the introduction of legislative ballances [*sic*] and checks—the institution of courts composed of judges, holding their offices during good behavior—the representation of the people in the legislature by deputies of their own election—these are either wholly new discoveries or have made their principal progress towards perfection in modern times.

These means for improving republican government received their fullest expression and strongest defense during the seventeenth and eighteenth centuries. These are also some of the theoretical elements of our constitutional system that were rejected by Schattschneider.

John Locke, Baron de Montesquieu, and Algernon Sydney were some of the early and main developers of this new science. But they were not the sole developers; our constitutional founders added an element to it, and to Schattschneider and others it was the crucial element. Publius continued:

> I shall venture, however novel it may appear to some, to add one more, on a principle which has been made the foundation of an objection to the new Constitution; I mean the ENLARGEMENT of the ORBIT within which such systems are to revolve, either in respect to the dimensions of a single state, or to the consolidation of several small states into one great Confederacy.

While the element of the new science of politics "discovered" by the American founders was the most controversial at that time, it proved to be the most sacred of these principles to Schattschneider. What he disliked about the new science was the earlier or European contributions, the ones that made our political system "the most complex system in the world."

It might be argued that it was the enlarged orbit of government that transformed the new science of politics into a uniquely American science of politics. The founders were steadfastly committed to the entire political system whereas Schattschneider and his followers felt the first three components of this system were detrimental to good, efficient government. It is with this fundamental disagreement in mind that we turn our attention to *Federalist* 10.

Schattschneider marveled at Publius's great insight into political parties given the fact that "Madison, though a veteran of factional politics in Virginia, had never seen a modern party in action when he wrote his essay." Schattschneider further noted Madison's recognition of the economic foundation of parties and their inevitability in a free society. But the inevitability of parties did not make them desirable to Madison or any of the other founders. Quite the contrary, Madison considered parties to be "inherently oppressive" and therefore in need of institutional devices to keep them from destroying popular government. On this issue, what Schattschneider ignored is far more important than what he addressed.

Schattschneider picked at the fringes of Madison's argument. He never cited Madison's definition of parties, nor did he develop Madison's discussion of the role economics played in party development. Had he done so, he might have avoided a fatal error in his own analysis of the founders' position on political parties. As is cited above, Madison had never witnessed a "modern party in action," nor had any of the other founders. For that reason, Schattschneider should have paid more attention to what Madison and others really meant when they referred to parties.

Had Schattschneider paid closer attention to the founders' own words on this subject, he might not have been so confused by what he perceived to be the "dual attitude" the framers of the Constitution had toward parties. On the one hand, he cited the founders' devotion to "the fundamental liberties in which parties originate." Then he quickly pointed out that they "set up an elaborate division and balance of powers within an intricate governmental structure designed to make parties ineffective."[5] If Schattschneider were not so limited in his own understanding of parties, he might have realized that the founders' scheme proved well suited to the kinds of parties that eventually developed in the United States.

What Madison and the other founders considered to be parties were the very "factional" groups they had dealt with in Virginia and other local regions. This was what permitted Madison and others to be experienced in factional politics and yet ignorant of modern political parties. That was also why Madison used the terms "faction" and "party" interchangeably throughout his argument. At that time no clear distinction existed between the terms "faction" and "party."

What Schattschneider identified as the founders' dual attitude toward parties was in fact their desire to frustrate factions, primarily economic factions, without placing barriers in the way of parties developed around ideas or more general public interests. Madison's two definitions of parties, the ones cited in my Introduction, help make this point. What was understood as a party in 1788 was something indistinguishable from a mere faction. Madison was not opposed to formal political parties; they had not yet been developed. Madison was describing and warning against factional groups like the interest groups of Schattschneider's day.[6] Like Madison, Schattschneider warned against the excesses of such groups in his book. In fact, Schattschneider concluded *Party Government* with as stern a warning against pressure groups as anything found in the early American documents.

The party prejudice Schattschneider brought to his analysis kept him from realizing the fundamental agreement he had with Madison on this all-important issue. In Chapter VIII when Schattschneider described pressure groups, he did little more than reveal how much more organized and structured Madison's factions had become. In his concluding chapter he argued that these pressure groups were one of the main threats to formal political parties; nothing in Madison's argument contradicts Schattschneider's conclusions about the baneful effects of pressure groups.

Schattschneider and other critics of the founders' views on political parties would have done well to note that the founders had no definite opinions about political parties in 1788 or 1789. Such political organizations had not yet existed. What the founders said about parties was generally their views on factions or interest groups. They were creating a system of government that would discourage the "mischief of faction" while permitting the open exchange of ideas that made political parties possible. This is what allowed Madison to pen the arguments in *Federalist* 10 and then organize the first genuine opposition party in America a few years later. The political party he helped form had nothing in common with the factions he decried earlier.

The Republican party Madison helped to create in the mid-1790s was a party built around clearly stated political principles. In fact, Madison's opening sentence in his party press editorial titled "Government of the United States" could not be more emphatic: "Power being found by universal experience liable to abuses, a distribution of it into separate departments, has become a first principle of free government."[7] It was a party that defended separation of powers and the federal system out of which it grew. It was a party developed to strengthen the constitutional system by helping facilitate the electoral system the Constitution created and to help organize the Congress the Constitution established.

The compatibility between Madison's political party and the Constitution existed because they both evolved from fundamental political principles, not transient policies or personalities. Most, if not all, of the responsible reformers call for political parties that are built around and characterized by their attachment to a set of public policies that the voters are asked either to accept or to reject. The American Political Science Association's report "Toward a More Responsible Two-Party System" (1950) acknowledged this shift when it claimed:

> Popular government in a nation of more than 150 million people requires political parties which provide the electorate with a proper range of choice between alternatives of action.[8]

If the "action" is appealing to the voters then the party is held responsible for implementing those policies. The next election becomes a referendum on those policies; the party is judged on its success at implementing those policies and on the success of those policies. If the party fails to fulfill its campaign promises, the voters can reject it and let another party form the next government.

According to the responsible rhetoric, such a system is more democratic than the founders' system. This is also why the responsible reformers believed that political parties are central to a democratic system of government. Schattschneider's brief discussion of the relationship between American political parties and the American Constitution is illustrative of this point. In his chapter titled "Other Special Characteristics of the American Party," Schattschneider described the relationship that exists between parties and the Constitution. He listed the Constitution as one of a half-dozen different "Special Characteristics." Schattschneider made every effort to ensure that the Constitution did not appear too important to the American political system.

Schattschneider, as had Wilson, praised the founders for their courage and actions while criticizing their work. He had to limit his praise because he was not happy with the overall system that grew out of the Constitution. Schattschneider's discussion of the Constitution occurs well beyond the midpoint in his book, yet he boldly maintained that his book "is devoted to the thesis that the character of the American party system is profoundly influenced by the Constitution of the United States."[9] He followed this surprising mid-volume thesis with the assertion that "no attempt will be made to defend the thesis as an exclusive explanation." Indeed. Nothing in the preface or the first chapters of *Party Government* would lead one to believe that this was his thesis. Even in books, actions can speak more loudly than words.

Nevertheless, what he had to say about the Constitution is of importance. He revealed his understanding of the relationship between the two when he observed:

> If the parties are the river of American politics, the stream of the living impulse to govern, the Constitution is the river bed, the firm land whose contour shapes the stream. In the long run the river can transform the landscape, but it is also the prisoner of the land. To study the parties as if they operated in a constitutional vacuum, apart from the institutions through which they must work, is futile, but alas it has been done![10]

It is easy to question the sincerity of Schattschneider's assertion given the pathetic nature of it in terms of its timing and brevity. There is one revelation in the above quotation that rings true throughout his work. His river and land analogy describes the parties as a "prisoner" of the constitutional landscape. If this is the thesis of his book, then Schattschneider must have considered himself to be functioning as a lawyer appealing the prisoner's case in the hope of freeing the political parties from their unjust bondage.

Schattschneider quickly identified the main obstacles the Constitution poses to parties as separation of powers and the federal system. These cruel constitutional wardens are joined by other prison officials such as fixed terms for the president and Congress. Because of these constitutional features Schattschneider observed: "One is tempted to say that these provisions have made real party government impossible in the United States; what we have instead is an abortive attempt at party government."[11] But there really was no attempt at party government; the attempt was at constitutional government, an attempt that was far too successful for Schattschneider's liking. Schattschneider followed these observations with the typical "party government" praise of the British parliamentary system. Echoing many of Wilson's arguments, Schattschneider proceeded with a polemic against the American party system as a vastly inferior system when compared to its European counterpart. He wanted the American parties to be able to present a "united front" on public programs: "The opportunity to mobilize the public behind a program is therefore wasted."

The desires of responsible party reformers have been for a stronger party system, but it is not a stronger American party system. They advocate stronger parties but not of the American variety. What they desire would be just as destructive of the American party system as anything advanced by the antiparty reformers.

We must further realize that the call for party government means, quite intentionally, the demise of constitutional government, at least as most Americans understand that term. The American constitutional system, developed in conformity with the new science of politics, was designed to bring stability to popular government. The complex system of auxiliary precautions makes our political system slow and deliberate; these were the very characteristics that made popular government acceptable in the 1780s.

James MacGregor Burns, one of the responsible champions I discuss later, described what the founders were trying to accomplish with these auxiliary precautions when he noted: "The fact is that Madison believed in a government of sharply limited powers." This was a great sin to Burns because it "meant weaker government."[12] He was absolutely right. The founders' scheme was so successful that Burns and the rest of the responsible reformers failed to recognize the lessons that had guided the founding generation, the lessons that had made democratic governments an impractical political option to every responsible political figure prior to these "inventions of prudence."

The temptation to call the responsible reformers the "rediscoverers of imprudence" is great. Party government advocates desire a more active government, but they seem incapable of acknowledging energetic government within the founders' constitutional setting.[13] In actuality, these reformers have called for dismantling all the devices Publius labeled the "inventions of prudence." Developing our case requires that we look carefully at the kinds of changes the responsible reformers have advocated. Since these reformers are such a diverse group,[14] we will focus our attention on three of the most influential proposals to come from the movement: Schattschneider's *Party Government*, the American Political Science Association's report "Toward a More Responsible Two-Party System," and James MacGregor Burns's *The Deadlock of Democracy*.

As has been noted, Schattschneider was at the forefront of the mid-century revival and, for that reason, he focused most of his attention on "the problem." Nevertheless, he does provide some general suggestions for strengthening political parties.

At the beginning of his concluding chapter, Schattschneider described the three "principal forms of political organization" in America. He argued that these three forces were involved in a "triangular tug of war"; each group represented radically different visions of America and none of these visions was consistent with the true national interest. He identified presidential parties as the most unifying of the three forces, but all were inadequate contenders for mobilizing a national majority. The development of presidential parties had been one of the positive contributions to American government of political parties in general. Nevertheless, while Schattschneider admired both the centralizing influence of presidential parties and the extent to which they helped simplify the American political system, he feared the dictatorial results that would occur if this influence continued unchecked.[15]

The other two "principal forms of political organization" provided the only real check on presidential parties. These were the local party bosses and the pressure groups. The problem with these two groups was that they checked the presidential parties without offering any real policy alternatives. Their interests were too local or too narrow to guide the country. Yet they were the only two forces competing with the presidential parties in the "war of extermination for supremacy in Congress."

According to Schattschneider, the only thing worse than maintaining the "static equilibrium" that existed among the three groups would be for one of them to gain dominion over the other two. Our only salvation from the paralysis of stalemate or the tyranny of no stalemate would be the establishment of party government.[16] "As mobilizers of majorities the parties have claims on the loyalties of the American people superior to the claims of any other forms of political organization."[17] Beyond this, party government is preferable to the alternatives because it is backed by the "great moral authority of the majority," an authority none of its rivals can claim.

Interestingly, when Schattschneider developed the case against the other forms of political organizations, his discussion focused only on pressure groups and local bosses. Clearly, his plan envisioned party government's taking the place of presidential parties in the three-way struggle for political dominion. He defended this replacement by asserting:

> The best antidote for the kind of paralysis that invites thoughts about dictatorship is party government, as distinguished from mere party controversy ending in frustration. Party government is the democratic and liberal solution of the problem of reconciling authority and liberty, for the parties can govern without destroying liberty; they can manage interests without becoming oppressive.[18]

Schattschneider further believed that the barriers to establishing party government were not insurmountable. He claimed: "The greatest difficulties in the way of the development of party government in the United States have been intellectual, not legal." Once we overcome the intellectual "difficulties" that stand in the way of party government, "party government will facilitate the solution to the greatest constitutional problems."

Schattschneider identified the greatest constitutional problems as the "problems of constitutional centralization." A centralized party system would facilitate the correction of some of these problems and obviate others. The most urgent need was to unify and centralize Congress. Schattschneider's argument, in one respect, was reminiscent of Madison's: "a tendency toward a presidential dictatorship can be dissolved in a strong national party system of leadership."[19] Madison's rhetoric was not as strong when he was organizing congressional opposition to Alexander Hamilton's executive plans, but the spirit of his activity was the same. Schattschneider broke with Madison because he did not see such leadership as a supplement to our constitutional system, but as a substitute for it. He ended his call for strong party leadership by arguing that "political responsibility is more flexible, comprehensive, and powerful than the system of legal responsibility set up in the separation of powers."

Schattschneider was every bit as uncomfortable with separation of powers and the legal system that maintained it as was Croly; he differed from Croly only as to the means deemed necessary to free us from this legal incarceration. To help address the intellectual problem of establishing a party government, Schattschneider turned to the American Political Science Association. Schattschneider chaired the Committee on Political Parties which produced the well-known report titled "Toward a More Responsible Two-Party System." This report is theoretically consistent with what we have observed in *Party Government*, but it differs from the earlier work by being much more specific. It also focuses more directly on an observation made at the start of Chapter Three about the distinction between responsible government and responsible parties.

The committee's report is quite obviously just that—a committee report. It is organized like a military instructional manual: it outlines what points will be covered, it covers those points, and then it concludes by restating those points. The report's carefully organized outline format is as systematic as it is confusing.[20]

The first paragraph of the report indicates that political parties need to place greater emphasis on public policy than they have in the past, an emphasis the committee believed to be mandated by the "very operations of modern government." The committee further indicated the kind of party system that is needed: "The party system that is needed must be democratic, responsible and effective."[21] On the committee's horizon, parties cannot be democratic or effective without first being responsible.

The committee cited many reasons for these needed reforms within the party structure. In the final analysis, all the committee's reasons could be traced back to one major cause, the committee's belief that the founders' notion of limited government was outmoded:

> The expanding responsibilities of modern government have brought about so extensive an interlacing of governmental action with the country's economic and social life that the need for coordinated and coherent programs, legislative as well as administrative, has become paramount.[22]

The need for "coordinated and coherent programs" had taken the place of Roosevelt's call for "enlarged governmental clothing." Once again, it was the reformers' opinion that the founders' plan was poorly suited to the new, modern American society. The quotation by Burns cited earlier was a more direct way of stating the same thing.

The responsible party reformers still desired a new streamlined form of government. Unlike the Progressives, though, these reformers saw parties as the solution, not the problem. In fact, the faith they had in party reform was truly remarkable. They took to new heights the Progressives' belief in parties altering the Constitution. Yet the Committee on Political Parties was very ambiguous about what role constitutional reforms may have to play in altering the political system. The committee clearly hoped and expected that party reforms would alleviate the vague political problems they identified, but they never totally ruled out constitutional amendments as a means of correcting the political system. In one of the committee's first statements on this topic they claimed: "To amend the Constitution in order to create a responsible cabinet system is not a practicable way of getting more effective parties." Instead they argued: "The parties can do much to adapt the usages under the Constitution to their purposes."[23] The implication is clear: it is not that amendments are undesirable, only that they are "not practicable." Can party reform do all that is necessary to bring about the desired kind of government? The committee did not know for sure, but they believed that parties "can do much." This line of argument is developed more fully but no more definitively later in the report when it is explained:

> Actually the parties have not carefully explored the opportunities they have for more responsible operation under existing constitutional arrangements. It is logical first to find out what can be done under present conditions to invigorate the parties before accepting the conclusion that action has to begin with changing the constitutional system that did not contemplate the growing need for party responsibility when it was set up.[24]

Again, the committee did not rule out amending the Constitution, it only expressed a desire to explore party reforms first. When the committee discussed stronger party organization in Congress, they did state that a cabinet system might weaken communication between the president and congressional leaders.[25] It is at this point that the committee proposal for the creation of a Party Council takes on its fullest meaning. In many respects the proposed Party Council was viewed as the organization that would overcome most, if not all, of the problems caused by the fragmented and decentralized nature of the American party system. For that reason, the proposal is cited in its entirety:

> We propose a Party Council of 50 members. Such a Party Council should consider and settle the larger problems of party management, within limits prescribed by the National Convention; propose a preliminary draft of the party platform to the National Convention; interpret the platform in relation to current problems; choose for the National Convention the group of party leaders outside the party organizations; consider and make recommendations to appropriate party organs in respect to congressional candidates; and make recommendations to the National Convention, the National Committee or other appropriate party organs with respect to conspicuous departures from general party decisions by state or local party organizations. In presidential years, the council would naturally become a place for the discussion of presidential candidacies, and might well perform the useful function of screening these candidacies in a preliminary way. Within this Party Council there might well be a smaller group of party advisers to serve as a party cabinet.[26]

The Party Council, as described here and elsewhere in the document, would make an important unifying force for the national government.[27]

The Party Council would also recommend, interpret, and enforce the party platform; screen potential candidates; and level sanctions against those party units that were in "open rebellion against policies established for the whole party."²⁸

In the final analysis, the Party Council would provide an antidote to the problems created by separation of powers and federalism. This group would be the great political homogenizer of our political system and would surely become the real focal point of all political power. The implication of this entire discussion is that something similar to democratic centralism should evolve. The central position of the Party Council or the more elite Party Cabinet would ensure that an enormous amount of power and authority would gravitate to it. At that point, the need for constitutional reforms to overcome the inconveniences of institutional checks and balances would be obviated.

James MacGregor Burns shared the above opinion but approached the problem in a different way. For him the problem of party reform was quite simple: "The aim is to draw the congressional and presidential party leaderships to each other by drawing the two party electorates more closely together."²⁹ Like the committee report, Burns argued that the parties had the power to correct the problems that confronted American politics. Burns was probably closer to Wilson theoretically than any of the other reformers in this study. He shared Wilson's obsession with leadership; in fact, this is his final word in *The Deadlock of Democracy*:

> The cure for democracy, people used to say, is more democracy. A half century of hard experience has shown this cliche to be a dangerous half-truth. The cure for democracy is leadership—responsible, committed, effective and exuberant leadership.³⁰

Burns offered a six-point plan for creating this much needed leadership.

Much of what Burns called for was perfectly consistent with what was advocated by the Committee on Political Parties. Fortunately, he was more direct and better organized. The "specific elements of party consolidation" are as follows.

"1. The national government should control national elections."³¹ Burns argued that as long as national elections are controlled by states the constituencies for senatorial and congressional elections will remain "small, noncompetitive, and exclusive." A genuinely national party cannot tolerate such fragmentation.

"2. Political parties must build grass-roots memberships." Burns advocated parties with "card-carrying, dues-paying membership." He believed that such a change would make club activities more common within the national parties. These clubs would weaken the parties' dependence on committees and "encourage an open, vigorous, and policy-oriented politics." Burns looked to the national interest groups as a model, arguing that their national membership had transcended the old localism of the nineteenth-century machines. The Committee on Political Parties made a similar observation about the nationalizing influence of interest groups when they claimed: "They counteract and offset local interests. . . . Indeed, the proliferation of interest groups has been one of the factors in the rise of national issues because these groups tend to organize and define their objectives on a national scale."[32]

"3. The presidential and congressional parties must be merged organizationally." On this point Burns limited his discussion to the method used in organizing electoral ballots. Acknowledging that ballot format can influence voting, he argued that ballots should be structured so they highlight "the key relationship of President to Senators and Representatives."

"4. New party leadership must be developed in Congress." The main villain in this section is the seniority system which is described as an "institutional bases of minority and obstructionist politics." Burns called for bipartisan support from the two presidential parties to overcome the fragmentary rules in Congress. In place of the seniority system he would like to see congressional leaders elected by a party majority in each house. The congressional reforms that followed the 1974 election were certainly a step in this direction.

"5. The parties and their candidates should be financed on a mass, popular, systematic basis." The dues-paying membership advocated under proposal two would help with this financing. Burns also advocated placing limits on the amount of money an individual or family may contribute to a party. This limitation has largely been accomplished by campaign reforms passed since his book was published in 1963. The principle behind this argument is one that has been embraced in recent decades: "It is better that a lot of people give a little money than that a few give a lot."

"6. The national opposition party should be better organized and given a clearer voice." In addition to permitting the party to control a larger amount of money, Burns wished to see the party meet more regularly. The party out of office especially needs regular meetings so it can provide a critique of the policies of the party in power. He believed that the national chairman of the out party should be the "acknowledged spokesman" for that party.

All of these proposals were designed to provide a clearer national voice for both political parties. In the interest of a clearer national agenda and platform, he wanted the two presidential parties to gain a controlling hand over the congressional parties. Clearly the federal structure of the American party system is as much an obstacle to his objectives as the system of separation of powers.

While Burns argued that constitutional changes were not necessary to bring about the desired changes, he acknowledged three that "would be extremely helpful." The first would allow election of representatives for four-year terms. This would make their terms coincide with presidential terms. The obvious purpose for this would be to tie representatives more closely to the presidential party. The second change would be the repeal of the Twenty-second Amendment. This would not only permit a longer ongoing relation between the president and Congress, but would also strengthen the presidential party. The third change would abolish the Electoral College. Burns saw the Electoral College as an institution that tied presidential elections too closely to the fragmented congressional parties. While he was not firmly committed to any particular alternative, he desired freeing the presidency from the politics of gerrymandering.

As desirable and helpful as these amendments might be, Burns warned against letting them divert our attention from the "more central need of party and governmental reform."[33] This last point placed Burns squarely within the responsible party camp. Schattschneider, the Committee on Political Parties, and Burns all believed that it was within the realm of party reformers to alter fundamentally the nature and focus of the American political system. The Constitution could be amended in ways that would be helpful, but real reform was the responsibility of the political parties.

The responsible reformers' desire to have parties overcome constitutional inconveniences was a leap of faith that would have made Croly proud. All of these responsible reformers considered the Constitution to be a major source of American political fragmentation. Yet they did not consider it to be an important part of the solution. It could also be that they did not want to take on the exceedingly difficult task of opposing our founding generation. This might explain why Burns went to such great lengths to argue that two competing and contradictory political systems grew out of the founding era. He argued that a strong party system could be traced back to what he labeled the Jeffersonian system.

Burns's effort to link Thomas Jefferson to a majoritarian party system, in contrast to what he described as Madison's anti-majoritarian system of checks and balances, was clever. Unfortunately, he took considerable liberties with the actual political history of the age. Madison, as has been noted earlier, was the mastermind behind both political systems and he felt that they were perfectly compatible, even complementary. It could be that the failure of the responsible party advocates was caused as much by their lack of a clear historical perspective as it was by their unwillingness to accept the Constitution as an important political document.

Chapter Five

Encouraging the Mischief of Faction

When our forefathers decided to "dissolve the Political Bands" which had connected us to Great Britain, they did so arguing that the only just powers of government are derived "from the Consent of the Governed." The patriots of 1776 felt so strongly about this conviction that they were willing to pledge their lives, their fortunes, and their sacred honor in defense of this principle of consent. The actions of our revolutionary forefathers supported Thomas Jefferson's claim that the Declaration of Independence was an "expression of the American mind." While American history reveals periods when the extent and nature of that consent were debated, no serious American statesman or responsible American citizen questions the validity of this basic truth.

And yet, accepting this statement as true in theory and knowing how to perpetuate its truth in practice are quite different matters. Considerable attention has focused on this question in recent years within the Democratic party. Some reform efforts have taken place within our legislative chambers but the lion's share of the discussion of consent has focused on the executive branch—more specifically, on the method used by the Democrats when selecting the delegates to their presidential nominating convention. Most historians and political scientists designate 1968 as the year when the Democrats started their political soul-searching. In fact, the Democrats began examining the nature of consent within their delegate selection process in 1964; a good case can be made for the whole process beginning with the credentials challenge to the Mississippi delegation at their 1964 convention.

The Democratic party worked out a compromise solution to the conflict between the "regular" Democratic delegates from Mississippi and the Mississippi Freedom Democratic Party delegates. In addition, the convention established a Special Equal Rights Committee to meet after the 1964 convention. This committee examined the rules and procedures of the

Democratic party, met with state party officials, and held public hearings. The culmination of its work was a report presented to the Democratic National Committee in the fall of 1967.

The report, "Second Report of the Special Equal Rights Committee," outlined six steps the party should take to avoid "discrimination on the grounds of race, color, creed, or national origin."[1] But racial discrimination proved to be a minuscule tip on a gargantuan reform iceberg. The extent of the problem confronting the Democratic party was described by the Hughes Commission in 1968. This often forgotten commission described the real threat to the Democratic party in its report to the Rules Committee of the 1968 convention. The fact that this report had little impact on the turbulent 1968 convention does not diminish its importance to the party's reform efforts. The importance of this report is twofold: first, it provides a clear statement on what many believed to be the problem that confronted the Democratic party in the mid–1960s; second, it may rightfully claim to have set the tone for the much-better-known McGovern-Fraser Commission.[2] These are obviously interrelated. The Hughes Commission set the stage for the McGovern-Fraser Commission by giving some institutional legitimacy to the reform mentality and by making a compelling case in its assessment of the mid–1960s Democratic crisis.

The Hughes Commission's report, *The Democratic Choice: Report of the Commission on the Democratic Selection of Presidential Nominees*, also provides some insight into what was behind the Mississippi delegation challenge in 1964. The Hughes Commission's task was to make "recommendations for bringing the nomination process more closely into harmony with essential democratic principles."[3] According to Alexander Bickel, a member of the commission, this was an extremely important charge. Americans' faith in national conventions was at a low point in 1968, such a low point that talk of setting up a national primary election to take the place of the party conventions was being taken seriously. Bickel argued:

> This radical cure would put a premium on personal wealth and demagogic or irrelevant appeal. Moreover, national primaries would severely strain the two-party system. They would, in sum, come to a politics of ideological and charismatic fragmentation rather than of coalition and accommodation.

Bickel further stated:

> What the convention needs is not radical, but intelligently conservative, reform, aimed at enhancing both its representative nature and its deliberative, decision-making function.[4]

But it is not clear that what the Democratic party was calling for was intelligently conservative reform. The Hughes Commission itself called for some fairly sweeping reforms, and what it advocated was greatly expanded by the McGovern-Fraser Commission and by the states' interpretation of what compliance with the latter commission required. But compared to the "radical cure" of congressionally mandated primaries, almost any internal party solution might seem conservative.

The Hughes Commission's great accomplishment was that it clearly and honestly identified the two problems that confronted the Democratic party. The first might be described as a procedural problem: the commission "concluded that state systems of selecting delegates to the National Convention and the procedures of the Convention itself, display considerably less fidelity to basic democratic principles than a nation which claims to govern itself can safely tolerate."[5] The second problem was clearly political: the breaking up of the New Deal coalition.

The solution to the first problem was a matter of making the conventions more democratic. The commission believed this message was clear even before the turbulent 1968 convention had commenced: "As delegates assemble for the 1968 Democratic National Convention, the demand for more direct democracy and the call for an end to 'boss control' of the nominating machinery can be heard, with an intensity not matched since the Progressive Era."[6] How they would achieve greater democracy was yet to be decided, but even more difficult was determining whether greater democracy would be an appropriate antidote to their second problem.

The Hughes Commission's description of the factors causing the breakdown of the New Deal coalition certainly implied that greater democracy (direct democracy, to use its term) alone would not solve the second problem. The commission's description is such a vivid depiction of the kind of soul-searching that was going on within the Democratic party that it must be quoted in its entirety. Keep in mind, this statement was made before, not after, the disastrous 1968 convention.

Two distinct trends have produced the strains in the [New Deal] coalition. First, Negroes display a rapidly increasing dissatisfaction with the role of junior partners in the coalition; they are no longer content to permit whites to monopolize the positions of political power in the cities. Their demands for political power have brought them into conflict with many party leaders and organizations in Northern states. Their demands for far-reaching social and economic advances have created bitter conflict between themselves and the white ethnic masses who form the specific constituencies of white urban Democratic leaders. Meanwhile, Negro demands for civil rights and the support for those demands by the Northern liberal wing of the Party, have alienated the once Solid South and dropped the black belt from the list of states that could be counted on, or even hoped for, on the Democratic side in presidential elections.

Concurrent with the Negro revolution, changes in its white components have undercut the potency of the New Deal coalition. The electorate is generally more affluent and more widely educated. The descendants of early twentieth century immigrants have now spread to all reaches of the economic spectrum; their voting patterns tend to reflect their economic status as much or more than their ethnic and religious background. They can no longer be counted on to vote Democratic, especially as far as the presidency is concerned.[7]

In sum, the commission saw the Democrats' problems as ethnic and economic. One group was no longer content to ride in the back of the bus and another either did not want to share the front seats with them or were now in a position to use private transportation. One problem produced party conflict; the other, party abandonment. While this assessment was probably fairly accurate, it was not very reassuring for the Democratic party.

The raised expectations that produced discontent were, in many ways, the product of the Great Society programs. So it might be argued that the Democrats of the late 1960s were the victims of their own success. They described that problem in the following way: "the increasing education and affluence of the electorate generally have combined to erode substantially the role of well-defined interest groups in presidential politics." Education and affluence have weakened "well-defined interest groups" by producing "issue-oriented individuals who rank relatively abstract ideological questions high among the criteria by which they approve or disapprove of candidates."[8]

The reforms that followed the Hughes Commission's report were not consistent in reflecting the perceived shift away from interest group politics to issue-oriented politics. The commission's findings did not produce uniform results. Some groups were still treated as interest groups; they had not achieved the "issue-oriented independence" that others had. Presumably, this was because they lacked either the education or the affluence that would permit them to be more issue oriented and independent. Even more surprising, the number of groups that receive special treatment from the party has grown considerably since 1972.

In many respects the reform Democrats of the late 1960s and early 1970s were following the lead of their Progressive predecessors. They echoed the Progressives' call for greater democracy and their attack on "boss rule," but, more importantly, they also considered the nominating conventions to be a major villain. This should not surprise us since both reform movements were the direct result, at least partially, of reformers' dissatisfaction with the outcome of a particular nominating convention. William Howard Taft's victory in 1912 and Hubert Humphrey's in 1968 were made possible, in the reformers' eyes, by undemocratic procedures in the conventions. Both nominations also led to a series of reforms that have had a major impact on our two-party system.

Reforming the national party system means reforming the presidential selection process. This, in turn, means reforming the party convention system. While there have been some efforts to abolish party conventions in this century, these have all failed. In 1968 the congressional efforts to set up national primaries were defeated because of the Democrats' sweeping reforms. Here again, the Hughes Commission performed an admirable service by clarifying the purpose and role of party conventions. It began its examination of the topic by observing:

> The key to selecting a presidential nominee who is genuinely the people's choice lies with the states. If delegations to the national convention are not chosen democratically even the most admirably structured convention will not be democratic. Conversely, if state delegations are democratically selected, efforts to "rig" the convention will probably fail.[9]

In addition to this, the commission added: "Virtually the only valid purpose of state delegate selection is representation of popular preferences or, more precisely, representation of the first preferences of the people." But the commission was quick to add that the purpose of the convention must go beyond "the first preferences of the people." While the representative function is of central importance to any convention, it is not the sole function. Indeed, if that were, it would be hard to defend nominating conventions. The "first preferences of the people" could be represented by some kind of national or regional primary system, completely bypassing nominating conventions.

The Hughes Commission's confused yet unswerving commitment to conventions was based on what it described as the "additional aims" of the convention:

> Yet the convention must serve additional aims. Since there are often more than two candidates in the running for a party's nomination, none may be able to win a majority on a first-ballot polling of the delegates. Furthermore, the position of the various candidates on matters of ideology and policy may be ambiguous or flexible—subject, therefore, to modification according to the power or weakness of the various interests and elements represented by the party membership. When more than two candidates are running and none garners a majority on the first ballot, a convention must resolve the deadlock

by going beyond representation to the techniques of bargaining and deliberation.[10]

So, in addition to representing the will or preferences of the people,
party conventions must also function as a bargaining and a deliberative
body. The bargaining and deliberative functions encompass a good deal
more than just presidential nominations. No doubt, presidential nomination is the convention's first function, but there are a number of important
secondary functions involved as well. Here again, it is hard to improve on
the Hughes Commission's own words:

> A national party convention also serves an important ancillary purpose. The
> convention is the party's most useful single occasion for education of the
> electorate regarding the appeal of its candidate, other leaders and the posi-
> tions on policy which it espouses. Properly understood, the aim of education
> should serve not merely the party as a corporate entity, but also the various
> constituent interests, groups and factions which have particular points to ex-
> plain and dramatize.[11]

This last point is not a trivial one. The importance of education to this or
any other democracy is beyond question. One might argue that primaries
educate the public as well, but education is not a high priority for the
public relations firms that are hired to package a candidate.

The Hughes Commission established the four "primary roles of delegates" to a nominating convention as (1) representation, (2) bargaining,
(3) deliberation, and (4) education. While a particular convention may not
perform all four of these roles as well as the delegates might like, conventions are still the only vehicle the party has to perform these important
duties. The alternatives to nominating conventions, as we have heard for
over a century and a half from distinguished Democrats as diverse as Martin Van Buren and Bickel, place a higher premium on "demagoguery and
irrelevant appeals" than on constructive discourse. Primaries, as the main
alternative, may be representative, but they afford little or no occasion for
bargaining and deliberation, and have proved to be very weak educators
as well.

An additional task performed by conventions, one that is overlooked by
the Hughes Commission, is building the infrastructure of the party. Van
Buren considered this to be one of the great virtues of party conventions;
in fact, the development of our national party system was initiated with
the birth of party conventions. This is no historical coincidence. There
were political parties in America before the development of the party convention, but they were state parties. The only national parties that existed
were congressional parties, and should not be confused with the popular

national parties we have today. The Congressional or King Caucuses nominated party candidates for the presidency because there was no alternative. When national party conventions were created, there was finally a vehicle for drawing the different state organizations together to form a truly national party structure. So it is important to realize that presidential nominating conventions are an essential component of our national parties. To put it another way, every action that weakens national conventions weakens national parties just as much.

By overlooking the convention's role in building the party infrastructure, the commission set the party on a reform course that ultimately had grave consequences for the Democratic party—consequences that have baffled the party for more than two decades. A second problem that grew out of the Hughes Commission was its inability clearly to define the "essential democratic principles" to which it claimed such allegiance. This posed a theoretical problem for later commissions and the party in general. Indeed, I believe this has proved to be the central problem to plague the Democratic party since the factional reformers gained control of the party commissions. The Democratic party still has not settled on a clear definition of these "essential democratic principles."

The Hughes Commission made its recommendations to the 1968 convention: it urged the creation of another commission "to aid the state Democratic parties" in structuring reforms and then report back to the 1972 convention. Unfortunately, its recommendations were too mild for the turbulent convention which decided to follow the lead of the minority report of the Rules Committee. Aiding state parties was not what the minority report had in mind:

> They proposed that the 1972 Convention "shall require," in order to give "all Democratic voters . . . full and timely opportunity to participate" in nominating candidates, that (1) the unit rule be eliminated from all stages of the delegate selection process and (2) "all feasible efforts [be] made to assure that delegates are selected through party primary, convention, or committee procedures open to public participation within the calendar year of the national convention."

The commission that was created by the adoption of this report was the McGovern-Fraser Commission. This commission saw its creation as "an unquestionably stern mandate for procedural reform."[12]

The McGovern-Fraser Commission was, no doubt, correct in its assessment of the will of the more vocal elements of the Democratic party. Like the Hughes Commission, its rhetoric was perfectly consistent with the Progressive rhetoric that was heard some sixty years earlier. "For Democrats the way was clear: 'The cure for the ills of democracy,' it was long ago said, 'is more democracy.' '''[13] It is clear from the deliberations at the 1968 convention, and the endless series of commissions that the party has created since then, that "more democracy" means—first and foremost—more democracy as it is defined by the Democratic National Committee and its many commissions.

The one consistent result of all the reforms, the initial reforms and the reforms of the reforms, has been the destruction of state control over their delegate selection processes.[14] To be sure, the commissions have all claimed that states are free to use any of the three officially sanctioned procedures for selecting their delegates: convention, committee, or primary. Yet the rules that govern any and all of the systems have ensured that the real power within the Democratic party rests not with the states but with a collection of national commissions and committees like the Compliance Review Commission (now the Compliance Assistance Commission), the Rules Committee, the Credentials Committee, etc. By their standards, the states are incapable of democracy without some fairly narrow and detailed guidelines from the national organization. While this may not have been its intention, the Supreme Court has reinforced this notion in a number of cases, the best known of which is probably *Cousins v. Wigoda* (1975).

In the late 1960s and early 1970s, democratization meant getting the professional politicians out of the process and giving the rank-and-file party members greater control of the conventions. The professional politicians who were usually excluded were the loyal state party members and elected officials at all levels of government. The attack on professional politicians was in many respects a more specific attack on Southern, urban, and labor Democrats. We must not forget that during this same period congressional reformers were assailing the seniority system within their committee structure. Most observers recognized that the desire for greater democracy within Congress was really an effort to weaken the control entrenched Southern politicians had on key committees. Here again, the rhetoric of greater democracy was disguising the real battle over regional differences within the party.

Any regional bias or prejudice that existed within the party is, to a large extent, a secondary issue. Of greater importance is the fact that the Democratic National Committee and its commissions were (and certainly still are) actively involved in a major power struggle with the states. The national party's victories, however, have been internal victories which have led to a series of external defeats. The reformed Democratic party has not fared well in presidential elections. It could be argued that the

Democrats have reformed themselves into a minority party in presidential elections.

Since their reforms started in 1968, the Democratic party has won only two presidential elections. In 1976, the Democrats were able to elect Jimmy Carter to the White House, yet he proved incapable of governing during his one term in office. Many Democrats realized that Carter's problems in governing were caused, at least in part, by the fact that the electoral process had little resemblance to the governing process. The old nominating process required that candidates for the party's nomination establish political ties with key state and congressional leaders, the very people they would have to work with if they succeeded in their quest for the White House. The new nominating process discouraged establishing these important political ties. In fact, the grass-roots-oriented nominating process that evolved after 1968 seemed to favor those politicians who campaigned against professional politicians.

As noted earlier, it is still too early to know what Bill Clinton's election will reveal about the electoral process. During the 1988 and 1992 presidential elections, only minor revisions were made in the Democrats' convention rules. The Democrats' victory in 1992 may provide a continued deterrence to any major adjustment to the existing system. However, this may not serve their long-term interests.

It is hard for an elected official to build a good working relationship with Congress when the electoral system rewards those who attack Congress. The dislike for professional politicians that shaped the interest group reform era fostered convention rules with a built-in bias for those candidates who professed a similar dislike. Carter was a Washington outsider and dwelt heavily on this fact during his campaign. This may have been an electoral virtue but it was a governing vice. Clinton was an outsider as well, but this was not an important theme in his campaign. Quite the contrary, he argued that putting a Democrat in the White House would end gridlock and bring about political "change."[15]

The Democratic party's reforms placed so much distance between the party's nominee and the rest of the party that once the Democrats were able to capture the White House they were unable to do anything but damage their own cause. The Democrats' inability to govern effectively from 1976 to 1980 produced a major Republican victory in 1980. The American people were so dissatisfied with the Democrats that the Republicans not only regained the presidency in 1980, but captured a majority in the Senate as well. So far, Clinton has made every effort to keep history from repeating itself.[16]

The reform Democrats' obsession with representation at the expense of all other considerations has been noted. But they did not want representation of the simple "one man, one vote" variety. In fact, here they clearly broke from their Progressive forebears. The Progressives saw no reason to institutionalize interest groups. For the Progressives, people were people regardless of race, religion, or national origin. Progressives gave all people credit for seeing their group interest (if they felt attached to one), as well as the national interest, and voting accordingly. Interest groups were measured by their ability to mobilize their rank-and-file membership on election day. On this point, the Progressives were in total agreement with the founding generation.

Patronizing interest groups was simply not the Progressives' style. Interest groups are, of course, a real and permanent part of our political system, but there is a difference between drawing these groups into a larger coalition and simply trying to placate them. Nelson Polsby describes this as the difference between "building coalitions" and "mobilizing factions."[17] He then spends some time explaining why our constitutional system was structured so that coalition building would be possible, which was primarily to discourage the excesses of factions.

James Madison's scheme for "discouraging the mischief of faction" is, no doubt, the classic statement on why democracies should be suppressing, not mobilizing factions. Political parties help mitigate some of the negative aspects of factions by drawing them into a larger coalition, the very process for creating democratic majorities that can have lasting impact on the government. This approach also strengthens and enlightens both the interest groups and the general public. Conversely, attempts at placating interest groups simply reward those groups for not conforming or cooperating with the larger good of a party or community. Appeasing interest groups may be the easy way out in the short term, but in the long run it destroys majority rule. In place of the majority, we find the feudal lords of organized interest groups, each of whom possesses an item veto over party policies that may affect their narrow interests.

The theoretical model for this interest group veto is, of course, John C. Calhoun's concurrent majority thesis. Just like Calhoun before them, the Democratic factional reformers were trying to break up majority rule because it did not serve their immediate interest. One big difference between Calhoun and the latter-day reformers is that Calhoun understood the theoretical implications of what he was proposing. He did not claim to be advocating openness and direct democracy; he fully realized that factional checks on majority rule were a way to protect the interests of elite or special groups.

Did the Democratic factional reformers realize what they were doing?

If so, why were they hostile to majority rule? There was a small corps of hardline reformers who were keenly aware of what they were doing and, as often happens, they worked hard to secure key positions within the reform commissions so they could manipulate the process to serve their radical objectives. In the name of openness and democracy, a small group of antiparty reformers managed to seduce the rest of the Democratic party into following their lead. (No, this was not what they meant by "essential democratic principles.") The radical reformers were able to use the uncertainty which surrounded "essential democratic principles" to reshape the meaning of majority rule.

The McGovern-Fraser Commission began its study with some basic statements on the nature of the Democratic party. "We find common cause in our Party's history of fair play and equal opportunity." Accordingly, it was this heritage, the commission reasoned, that gave the Democratic party its "continuing vitality." For that vitality to continue, the party had to renew its commitment to "fair play and equal opportunity." There was no area of party affairs where this was more important than in the "choice of the party's presidential nominee." One could take this argument a step further and assert that the only national action taken by a party is its choice of a presidential nominee. So, of course, it is of the utmost importance to the national party.

But the party's concern for "fair play" raises another important question: Fair play for whom? The Winograd Commission pointed out part of the confusion that came over the party in the early years of reform. It is no secret why political parties are often the victims of a tug of war between competing factions. In its report titled *Openness, Participation and Party Building: Reforms for a Stronger Democratic Party*, the Winograd Commission identified the main contending factions within the Democratic party since 1968:

> Some define the Party as those activists and elected party officials that are involved with Party affairs year after year. They argue that these people should be well represented in the selection of a presidential nominee since it is their business to know and represent the electorate and to win elections.
>
> Reformers tend to define the Party as those voters who have enough of a psychological commitment to the Party to call themselves Democrats. They feel that it is most important to guarantee maximum grass roots involvement in the presidential nomination process.[18]

The factions competing for control of the Democratic party during the reform era were the "party officials" and the "grass-roots party." The reforms that began in 1968 had a decided preference for the latter group.

It was this preference that led to the expansion of presidential primaries among the states.

Presidential primaries have had their ups and downs throughout this century; what was novel about this most recent wave of primaries was the magnitude of the change:

> The number of states using primaries for selecting or binding Democratic national convention delegates increased from 17 in 1968 to 23 in 1972, 29 in 1976 and 31 in 1980. The percentage of all delegates chosen in these primaries went up from 38 per cent in 1968 to 75 per cent in 1980.[19]

While the move toward primaries was consistent with the reform spirit, some of the reform leaders expressed concern over this development. Donald Fraser, of the McGovern-Fraser Commission, favored a rule that would have set limits on the percentage of delegates who could be selected by primaries. James Ceaser points out that many reformers were hoping that the new rules would obviate primaries, yet many states switched to primaries "to avoid the great complexity that the new rules imposed in the case of caucus proceedings."[20] The states that maintained the caucus system found that the new rules had stripped away most of the advantages of that system.

The shift from party politics to reform politics within the Democratic party must be recognized for what it was. Byron Shafer, in his splendid work *Quiet Revolution: The Struggle for the Democratic Party and the Shaping of Post-Reform Politics*, claimed that it was the most radical shift in the presidential nominating process in American history. While I am not sure it was more radical than the development of the convention nominating process, it certainly was (and is) the most radical reform in the history of American political parties. It was also the most negative reform in American partisan history. This is true for two obvious and interrelated reasons.

First, conventions are what give political parties their national character. They are what link the diverse state party organizations in a manner that has historically benefited both the nation and the states. The states bring a statewide political network and a core of ready and able campaign volunteers to the party. The national organization provides media coverage and a national figure to present the party's position on major issues. The party's presidential nominee generally sets the tone for the campaigns at all levels. The electronic media only heighten this asset. While presidential coattails have not been very effective in recent years, the union between local organization and national inspiration has been the lifeblood of American's party system.

The reform Democrats of the 1960s actively worked to sever this vital link between the local organizations (including state organizations) and the national organization. Shafer's work makes it especially clear that these reformers were hostile to the very notion of an ongoing organization that brought stability to the electoral system. The reformers were far more interested in the psychological charge they received from challenging and disrupting "the system" than they were in the success the party might receive from a more stable and unified system. Shafer illustrates this when he observes that

> the ban on ex officio positions was only part of the general effort at the *separation of party officialdom from the delegate selection process,* and the preference for demographic groups over the regular party was more usefully seen in this light. In the vocabulary common to most other advanced democracies, many of the guidelines were, in fact, aimed at isolating *the party itself* from what was, at least rhetorically, "the party's nomination."²¹

The very political stability sought by Van Buren and others when they instituted the convention system was what the reformers disdained most.

The result was the destruction of the national Democratic party. The Democratic conventions ceased to be a unifying force for the party. Increasingly, the conventions were used to showcase the differences that existed within the party. Party conventions had historically functioned like pep rallies to charge up the party faithfuls and kick off the presidential campaign. The restructured factional reformed conventions functioned more like group therapy sessions than pep rallies. But this was probably just as well since the party faithfuls were no longer attending the conventions. The new delegates were social reformers first and Democrats second.

These reform delegates had little or no commitment to the principles that had shaped the Democratic party; they were not Jeffersonians, Jacksonians, or even New Dealers. They were instruments of change, and as long as the Democratic party accommodated change, they were Democrats.

The second reason I believe these reforms were negative is directly related to the first. By severing the tie between the presidential nominating process and the regular party organization, reformers ensured that the Democratic nomination would be a media event, not primarily, but exclusively. This enhanced the kind of politics Bickel argued against when he was on the Hughes Commission: "a politics of ideological and charismatic fragmentation rather than one of coalition and accommodation." Bickel advanced this warning when he was worried about a national primary system replacing the party conventions. He appears to have won the battle but lost the war.

Clearly, not all conventions are created equal. The factional reformers seemed perfectly comfortable with the old Progressive notion that "democracy should be defined not in terms of ends but in terms of means."[22] Where Madison argued in *Federalist* 51 that "justice was the end of government," these reformers would argue that democracy does not care about ends. It is not one's destination that matters, it is how comfortable the ride there. This is why I argued earlier that the party reformers of the past century were obsessed with means to the exclusion of ends. Abandoning justice as "the end of government" was probably an unexpected and unintended result of these reform efforts. But one cannot abandon the founders' concern for ends in general without abandoning the specific ends they hoped to achieve. The American founders viewed politics as a means to such ends as liberty and justice; latter-day American reformers view politics as an end in itself. For them, liberty and justice are not as important as procedural purity.

Chapter Six

The Harsh Reality of Reform

Democratic governments may not be orderly or neat, but they do have a way of putting things in perspective. As the Democratic reformers were busy dismantling their presidential party in 1969, the Nixons were rearranging the furniture in the White House. Richard Nixon had successfully appealed to the "silent majority" in America. His victorious campaign had been attributed to many things: the Vietnam War, urban unrest, liberal justices, to name just a few. One of the favorite reasons among Democrats was that Vice President Hubert Humphrey remained too loyal, too long to then-President Lyndon Johnson. Campaigning for the presidency while you are the incumbent vice president does have its liabilities.

One of the best explanations, one that more recent history certainly supports and one that the Hughes Commission was greatly concerned about, was the breakdown of the New Deal coalition. Franklin Roosevelt's coalition, like Abraham Lincoln's, Andrew Jackson's, and Thomas Jefferson's, was not destined to last forever. While the Democrats knew this, they also knew, or at least should have known, that majority coalitions are built around presidential candidates. The key to any political party's success is its ability to attract a candidate with the rhetorical skill to capture the country's heart and imagination. The key to any candidate's success is to have a formal organization that will reaffirm the message and interpret it to the rank and file.

The statesmen around whom coalitions are built are rare, but when they do appear they need a political party to support their message and weave it into the fabric of our political system. Jefferson's "revolution of 1800" carried the same message he had espoused in 1796. Although, during the four-year interval, a number of significant events had altered the political landscape, the critical difference between Jefferson's defeat in 1796 and his victory in 1800 was the organization that helped him advance his unchanged message.[1] Jackson's disappointment in 1824 was reversed in 1828 by the able organizational structure provided by Martin Van Buren and Thomas Ritchie.[2]

Alexis de Tocqueville, observing this phenomenon, noted in *Democracy in America*:

> All the skill of the actors in the political world lies in the art of creating parties. A political aspirant in the United States begins by discerning his own interest, and discovering those other interests which may be collected around and amalgamated with it. He then contrives to find out some doctrine or principle that may suit the purpose of this new association, which he adopts in order to bring forward his party and secure its popularity.[3]

What Tocqueville was describing is the party development we associate with critical or watershed elections. He had in mind these major realignments of the American electorate when he argued that "all the skill of politicians consists in forming parties." The Democratic party of the late 1960s should have put its energy into forging a new coalition, not dismantling the vehicle needed to do so. In the absence of a watershed election no new coalition has been formed.

Since the breakdown of the New Deal coalition, American politics has degenerated into factional fights or what Tocqueville called "small parties." The distinction Tocqueville made between "great" and "small" parties is helpful for understanding what emerged from the reform era. He distinguished between the two in the following way: "Society is convulsed by great parties, it is only agitated by minor ones; it is torn by the former, by the latter it is degraded; and if the first sometimes save it by a salutary perturbation, the last invariably disturb it to no good end."[4] This contrast fails to disclose the crucial difference between the two: "great" parties are those guided by principles; "small" parties are those guided by interests. The trouble caused by the destruction of the Democratic presidential party was especially unprofitable in the elections that followed.

America's party history indicates that most of the time our two major parties fall somewhere in between the extremes of "great" and "small." During these periods of relative political calm our main challenge seems to be one of keeping our parties cohesive enough so they do not degenerate into small parties.

The fundamentally important lesson from all this is that Tocqueville's small parties, James Madison's factions, and E. E. Schattschneider's pressure groups are all the same thing. In all three cases we are warned against the excesses of interest groups. But only Tocqueville and Madison recognize that the alternative to their divisive character and pettiness is a clear appeal to fundamental principles.

By 1980 or possibly 1978, the problems inherent in factional politics were beginning show in the Democratic party. The first institutional sign of some reservations by the party was the publication of the Winograd Commission report, *Openness, Participation and Party Building: Reforms for a Stronger Democratic Party*. The title itself reveals a radical departure from the obsession of earlier reformers. Remove the first three words from the title and we see the very thing earlier commissions had at best ignored and at worst declared open warfare against.

Any commission report that spends considerable time and energy developing a history is probably trying to stake out a new direction. At the very least, they want to keep open the possibility of moving in a new direction. Morley A. Winograd, chairman of the commission which carried his name, described the circumstances that might produce reconsidering the reforms at the 1980 convention: "If the President [Jimmy Carter] is successful [in his reelection], then you'll see very little [change in the nominating rules]. If the President is unsuccessful, and dramatically unsuccessful, then you'll see people looking at a whole lot of changes."[5] Carter was, of course, "dramatically unsuccessful" and the stage was set for rethinking the reforms.

Actually, the reforms were on very shaky ground before the final tally was in on the 1980 election. Michael Malbin observed that the Winograd Commission was being pulled by three distinct factions. One, led by both Carter and Edward Kennedy backers, was basically satisfied with the post-1968 reforms. A second group, which included a key player in the earlier reforms, Donald Fraser, was concerned about the proliferation of primaries. At one point Fraser suggested placing a cap on the number of primaries that could take place in any single nominating season. The third faction, guided by political scientists such as Austin Ranney, Jeane Kirkpatrick, and Thomas Mann, "wanted to increase the role of elected officials in conventions by getting more of them to attend as uncommitted delegates."[6]

What the Winograd Commission had been to the history of recent reforms within the Democratic party, the Hunt Commission (1982) was to the future of reform within the party. The Hunt Commission fairly accurately assessed the results of reform when it admitted:

Recent years have seen an electorate too often pulled to and fro by the issues and personalities of the moment. Executives and legislators alike have too often chosen to "go it alone" electorally; their accountability to the broad electorate and the overall coherence of government have suffered accordingly. Party politics—the politics of personal contact, deliberate judgement, coalition and compromise—have too often been replaced by remote-control campaigns, single-issue crusades, and faceless government.[7]

After acknowledging these rather obvious shortcomings the report further stated: "The traditional role of party—as a mediating institution between citizens and government, as a guide to consistent and rational electoral choice, and a bond pulling the elements of government together for the achievement of positive purposes—no longer seems secure."[8] Saying that a political party "no longer seems secure" in its ability to pull the government together in 1982 was a gross understatement. The two political branches of government had been openly hostile toward each other since the last years of the Johnson administration.

It is fitting that the commission which had dismantled the presidential party carried the names of two legislators. Senator George McGovern and Representative Fraser were both incumbent legislators when they began destroying the Democratic presidential party. A third legislator, Senator Eugene McCarthy, was, fittingly, the candidate who ran President Johnson out of the 1968 presidential campaign. The Republican party had reached a similar state of deterioration as well. In 1972, incumbent President Nixon established in practice what the Democrats had structurally accomplished through their commissions: a clean break between the presidential campaign and the rest of the party structure.

Nixon's Committee to Re-elect the President (CRP) not only ran independently of other Republican campaigns but actively against many. The Democrats for Nixon, chaired by then-Democrat John Connally of Texas, actively registered Democrats during the campaign and provided them with transportation on election day. The Nixon organization did not care who voters were voting for in gubernatorial races, Senate races, or any other campaign, as long as they were supporting Nixon for president. The importance of this action is often forgotten because of the more sensational Watergate scandal. But Nixon's 1972 campaign has become the model for all presidential campaigns since.

The Nixon approach to presidential campaigning affords candidates greater control over the campaign. This approach was institutionalized by post-Watergate reforms in campaign laws, the most important of which was public financing of presidential campaigns. This law ensures that every candidate has an independent campaign organization. It is ironic that the very campaign that led to major reforms in campaign laws established the model for the reformed campaigns.

Just as the campaign reform laws reinforce the Nixon model, they also reinforce the new independent Democratic structure as well. The unfortunate consequence of all these reform efforts was, and continues to be, the weakening of presidential coattails—coattails that are indispensable to watershed elections. The inability of either party to forge a new majority coalition has been the subsequent result.

What used to be healthy battles between major parties for the heart of the American electorate and the soul of American politics have become, regrettably, demoralizing little skirmishes between small parties over relatively obscure and largely administrative matters.

The most important battles of recent years have not been between partisans arguing over important principles, they have been between the political branches over technical questions about separation of powers. These can be important issues but the practical result of such struggles is less conclusive than a major realignment of the American voters. American voters may have opinions about these affairs but such affairs do not galvanize the citizenry. All too often where one stands on constitutional matters relating to separation of powers depends on the purely political consideration of which party controls which branch.

This last observation reveals yet another consideration. The breakdown of the national party structure does not mean that voters no longer have party allegiance. Quite the contrary, we are creatures of habit; unfortunately, party ties based on nothing stronger than habit contribute little to civic affairs. It also means that there is very little that can strengthen or weaken our party attachment. This is what makes a major realignment highly unlikely under such conditions.

The Democrats sensed these problems and started thinking seriously about rebuilding their presidential party after President Carter's unsuccessful bid for reelection. Winograd's prediction proved true. The Hunt Commission's first objective was to reestablish the link between those who attend the Democratic national convention and the more permanent elements of the Democratic party. To accomplish this reunification the commission recommended adding "approximately 550 slots" to the nominating convention "for the inclusion of party and elected officials as unpledged delegates."[9] These unpledged delegates are popularly called "superdelegates." Governor James Hunt Jr., the commission chairman, argued that superdelegates "will make the convention more representative of the mainstream of the party." Such a move was needed because "[w]e lost a lot of people in the last few years," he added.[10] This move had the additional advantage of restoring "peer" review to the nominating convention.

Another concern that had grown out of the 1980 convention was over what Kennedy called the "closed convention." Obviously his concern was not purely theoretical, but the issue stuck. Others were concerned that the delegates had no discretion once they arrived at the convention. Closed conventions, according to the Hunt Commission, "make the party and the convention less able to respond to a changing political environment."[11] With the addition of the superdelegates there would be a block of delegates free to vote their conscience. This would "restore a measure of decision-making flexibility and discretion to the national convention. . . ."[12]

The Hunt Commission acknowledged the role of primaries in the nominating process. Primaries help draw more people into the nominating process, "test grass-roots sentiment," and contribute to the number of candidate forums.[13] Despite the pluses, the commission saw the "critical shortcomings" as well. "Their proliferation has made for more protracted, more expensive, more divisive, and more media-dominated campaigns." Worst of all, primaries have "threatened to eclipse the organized party." The commission then provided information that suggests that caucuses actually produce a higher quality of participation. Their definition of higher quality means that more caucus participants will actually work for the party.[14]

All of these revisions in the reform rules were designed to "place a premium on coalition-building within the party prior to nomination and would promote a stronger party tie among our elected officials." This they hoped would "help make the Democratic party a strong and vital organization" that not only would be more competitive in the general election but might even have the capacity to govern, should the opportunity present itself.[15]

Winning elections and governing: should a political party really have to state these as important objectives? These are the very lifeblood of a political party. The need to express them as desirable goals reveals just how far the Democratic party had strayed. Expressing these goals, especially as forcefully as the commission did, had an important internal purpose. As noted above, three important factions existed in the Winograd Commission, but at first glance it would appear that only two of them survived the 1980 election. But this needs to be examined more carefully.

The happiest faction from the Winograd group would surely be the one that "wanted to increase the role of elected officials in conventions by getting more of them to attend as uncommitted delegates." Superdelegates, created by the Hunt Commission, were the direct result of their labors. In fact, what they were calling for in 1980 is as precise a definition of the superdelegates as you will find. But superdelegates were the creation of the Hunt Commission so we will look there for their description and rationale.

Superdelegates signaled the greatest retreat from the reform mood of the late 1960s and early 1970s. Their purpose was to get more party and elected officials back into the party conventions. The Hunt Commission described the rule change for convention delegates in the following manner:

> Each state will still have a 10% add-on for elected and party officials who are pledged to a candidate (or uncommitted) preference as it did in 1980. In addition, each state will have a larger add-on to be composed of unpledged delegates. The size of this add-on will be determined as follows: (a) each state will receive two slots for its Democratic Chair and Vice-chair; (b) 400 slots will be allocated to the states in proportion to the size of their base delegations; and (c) states for whom those allocations are insufficient to include their key Democratic elected officials (Governors, U.S. Senators, U.S. Representatives, Mayors of cities over 250,000 in population) will be granted additional slots sufficient to make the add-on equal to the number of such officials.[16]

This proposal was identified by the commission as the one that received the most "concentrated attention." This was the key ingredient for party building. They acknowledged and defended this honestly and directly.

> Why so much stress on increasing party and elected official participation? The Commission regards this as an important way to increase the convention's *representativeness* of mainstream Democratic constituencies. It would help restore *peer review* to the process, subjecting candidates to scrutiny by those who know them best. It would put a premium on *coalition building* within the Party prior to nomination, the forming of alliances that would help us campaign and govern effectively. It would *strengthen party ties* among officials, giving them a greater sense of identification with the nominee and the platform. And the presence of unpledged delegates would help return *decision-making discretion and flexibility* to the convention.[17]

No clearer statement could have been made about the crippling effects of the earlier reforms.

The superdelegates were so well received by the party that the Fairness Commission, the delegate selection advisory group for the 1988 convention, called for expanding the number of superdelegates and party official delegates to 24 percent of total delegates at the convention. The curious twist with this commission was the contrast between its origins and its results. The Fairness Commission was called for by the supporters of Jesse Jackson and Senator Gary Hart, mainly because of their dissatisfaction with the superdelegates. There were times when the superdelegates were all that kept Vice President Walter Mondale ahead of Hart during the 1984 campaign. Jackson realized that these delegates would never be in his camp. During the 1988 campaign Jackson called for distributing the super-delegates proportionally, a proposal that is hard to mandate when you are dealing with uncommitted delegates.

The results of the Fairness Commission were the opposite of what had been anticipated. As is noted above, superdelegates and elected and party official delegates increased between 1984 and 1988. There are two reasons for the turn of events. First, Hart probably reasoned that these delegates would be in his camp in 1988. Jackson was unsuccessful in getting the numbers reduced. The second reason for this change in results was the overall resurgence of the party regulars. There were too many elected and party officials on the commission, and their days on the outside looking in were over.

The next happiest faction must have been the group headed by Donald Fraser, then mayor of Minneapolis. This one-time reformer, though he was never part of the most radical wing of the movement, was concerned about the teeming primaries. The Winograd Commission sounded the first warning about potential problems with too many primaries.[18] The Hunt Commission established its position on primaries by observing: "Critics of the current trends generally do not see primaries as undesirable *per se*; the problem is rather an unbalanced *mix* of primary and caucus systems and the undue *weight* primary results have in determining the nomination outcome." These critics must have made their case to the commission because the final report concluded: "It is our conviction that it should be the policy of the national party to use whatever incentives and persuasive power it has at its disposal to encourage more states to shift from primaries to caucuses so that a better overall balance might result."[19]

Less obvious is how the third faction fared after the 1980 election. But there was one area of the early reforms that not only survived the revisionists' attacks but was strengthened. These were the "nondiscrimination" or "affirmative action" reforms. This is the one area where the Democratic party has been steadfast throughout its reform and revision periods. And, as noted earlier, this is the one area where they made the most radical departure from their Progressive forefathers.

The Democratic National Committee chairman of 1988, Paul Kirk, had made some changes at the DNC headquarters which indicated less pandering to caucus groups within the party. But the party rules reflected no fundamental change in the party's willingness to grant special privileges to certain groups. The rules governing this area are pretty confusing.

The McGovern-Fraser Commission called for each state to develop "affirmative steps to encourage" minorities, youth, and women to participate in the nominating process. The goal was for these groups to appear in the state's delegation "in reasonable relationship to the group's presence in the population of the State."[20] This proved to be a very confusing rule, for there was a footnote attached stating "that this is not to be accomplished by the mandatory imposition of quotas." A clear case of denying the obvious.[21] Many states considered the wording to mean quotas regardless of the footnote.

This is probably the thorniest of all the reform efforts and the one that has been the most unsettling. Additional rule changes proposed in 1978 reaffirmed the party's commitment to "a correlation between delegates and popular votes" and expanded the proportional test—or quotas—to Hispanics and Native Americans. The party also instituted an "outreach program" aimed at "groups such as ethnics, youths, persons over 65 years of age, workers [not one of the most clearly defined groups], persons with a high school education or less, the physically handicapped. . . ." Asian/ Pacific Americans were later added to the list, and then "persons of all sexual preference." Granting something like most favored nation status to an ever increasing number of groups made the party a virtual slave to special interests.[22]

With the development of the superdelegates, the party seemed to be saying that politicians were just another underrepresented group within the party. The Democrats' commitment to affirmative action is, indeed, the one area where there have been few, if any, second thoughts. The Hunt Commission made this very clear when it stated: "Our Party's affirmative action efforts are among the proudest achievements of reform. The Commission's action reflects our confidence in these programs, leaving their basic provisions intact while strengthening them in important respects."[23]

The party's unswerving commitment to affirmative action does not settle the confusion that surrounds the matter of quotas. The most awkward aspect is the one that appeared first in the Winograd Commission report. This commission established the "equal division clause," which mandates an equal division of men and women delegates at the convention. Despite the party's insistence that it did not want quotas, it created a quota for women. Since the commission gave in to interest group pressure on this issue it will be interesting to see what effect, if any, this will have over the long run with other groups.

A fair conclusion to draw from the post-1980 revisions is that the party is seriously committed to bringing the professional politicians back into the presidential party. The reestablishment of this link is, no doubt, necessary to the revival of the Democratic party and its electoral apparatus. As the election of President Carter made glaringly obvious, electing a candidate does not ensure that the party will be able to govern. One thing Carter illustrated was that even with bad rules and little or no party unity, it was still possible to win the presidency. To a large extent this is due to the role played by the mass media, especially television. No doubt Watergate was a factor as well.

The Carter years demonstrated something far more important than the Democrats' ability to win despite their self-inflicted wounds. What is accomplished with that victory has important long-term consequences. For this reason, the Hunt Commission saw party building as something that needs to occur on at least two levels. First, the commission wanted to reestablish the Democratic party "as a mediating institution between citizens and government, as a guide to consistent and rational electoral choice. . . ."[24] The medium of television establishes a link only between the citizens and the president. No other government official really has the access needed to use this medium effectively.

This is not only a myopic link, it has proved to be one that focuses more on form than substance. Television has never been "a guide to consistent and rational electoral choice." Even in televised presidential debates, which seem to be an established part of presidential elections now, we learn a good deal be more about what the journalists think is important than we do about the candidates. The candidates' three-to-five-minute "response time" simply does not allow a candidate to do more than establish an image.

National party conventions are the only real forum for establishing the principles and themes around which a campaign can be built. Furthermore, it is only when elected officials from all levels of government participate in setting those principles and establishing the themes that a truly national campaign is established. In a sense, it is the convention that gets all the party's candidates singing from the same hymnal.

The Hunt Commission did see mediation as linking only the government with the citizens. This is a necessary electoral and educational task, but is not enough. Parties must also mediate between and among the "elements of government." Only then can a party sufficiently perform the task of "governing effectively." Herein lies the real lesson of the Carter years.

A truly effective presidential campaign is not just one in which the party's candidate wins, it is also one that leaves the party in a position to effectively govern. To put this in Tocqueville's terms, minor parties may be able to win occasional victories but only great parties are capable of governing. Madison helps explain why this is the case in *Federalist* 49:

> If it be true that all governments rest on opinion, it is no less true that the strength of opinion in each individual, and its practical influence on his con-

duct, depend much on the number which he supposes to have entertained the same opinion. The reason of man, like man himself, is timid and cautious when left alone, and acquires firmness and confidence in proportion to the number with which it is associated.

Parties help provide the association that gives opinion the strength to take action.

Bringing professional politicians back into the presidential party is one giant step to reunification of the Democratic party. As noted, it permits the party to perform the important mediating function within the government. But de-professionalization was not the only move that destroyed the Democratic party's unity. The other factor which weakened the party was its encouraging the mischief of faction. And, as we have seen, there has been no reversal or retreat on this front.

The Democrats appear to be gambling that unity can occur with interest group representation provided they do not succumb to the pressure of addressing specific interest group policies. The 1988 Democratic convention rules and platform illustrate this shift. The 1988 convention was still straddling the quota-affirmative action fence. The rules for the 1988 Democratic convention continued to call for "outreach programs" which would include "recruitment, education and training" for such groups as youth, elderly (over 65), lesbians and gay men, workers, those with little or no education, blacks, Native Americans, Asian/Pacific Americans, etc. They continued to mandate an equal division between men and women for both delegate and alternate positions.

None of this was to be accomplished "either directly or indirectly by the Party's imposition of mandatory quotas at any level of the delegate selection process. . . ."[25] The Democrats appear to have dropped the "reasonable relationship" language and instead call for achieving "full participation of such groups in the delegate selection process." The language is not what is important on this issue; what is important is their belief in and commitment to interest group representation and the awkward way they deal with that issue. From convention to convention they must wrestle with hundreds of different groups trying to decide which are deserving of special consideration and which are not. Once they have decided who to include, they then must worry about the level of inclusion. "Non-Discrimination" is the lowest tier of preference, the next tier of preference is "Affirmative Action," and the highest level of preference is the "Equal Division" tier which so far has been granted only to women.

The importance of these layers of preference is not whether these groups should have a voice in government; of course they should. All citizens should have access to our political system unless they are legally prohibited from such participation. The problem with what the Democrats have been doing is that it encourages people to think of themselves as an interest group member first and a citizen second. This is what Madison was warning against in *Federalist* 10 when he warned against the "mischief of faction." He described factions or interest groups as "a number of citizens, whether amounting to a majority or a minority of the whole, who are united and actuated by some common impulse of passion, or of interest, adverse to the rights of other citizens, or to the permanent and aggregate interests of the community."

One of the problems with interest group representation is that it does place the group interest before the "permanent and aggregate interests of the community." When people attend meetings like party conventions as interest group representatives, they feel an obligation to represent that group's interest even if it is to the detriment of the larger good. There is the added disadvantage of subordinating the individual's own judgment to what is perceived to be the judgment of the group being represented. If you really want delegates to the national convention to be free to deliberate and show good judgment, you must free them from the shackles of the interest group.

Walter Berns explained the founders' aversion to interest group representation when he noted:

> The closest thing to group representation is in the Senate, where—in the words of *Federalist* 39—the states "as political and coequal societies" are represented; but every effort to represent property or family, as a means of balancing democracy, to say nothing of sect, nationality, language, color, or gender, was soundly defeated in the constitutional convention.[26]

Group representation is not only contrary to the founders' intentions, it is contrary to the common good as well as the sound judgment and self-esteem of the individual delegate. As such, it is also contrary to what the Democratic party says it is trying to do in its post-reform era. If the party is going to rally around some general principles and common themes, it must rise above the interest group mentality, something it is not likely to do as long as it encourages interest group representation.

Removing interest group policies from their party platform removes the facade of interest group dominion, but only through the removal of interest group representation can the reality be eradicated. A major realignment of the American voters cannot occur in a system dominated by interest groups. Tocqueville argued, rightfully it seems, that major parties can be forged only through appeals to principle. Such appeals are foreign to the interest group model of democracy.

Bringing politicians back into the convention is an important step in undoing the harm that was caused by the excesses of the radical reformers, but it will not revive the party's ability to govern. By now it should be clear that interest group politics is the politics of administration, not the politics of governing. Groups are concerned about governmental administration because they are tied into the bureaucratic structure either formally or informally; the great mass of American voters stay as far away from government bureaucracy as possible.

The factional reformers' dedication to interest group representation is what will keep them from building a strong presidential party. When Van Buren was building the presidential party system in the 1820s, he recognized the vital role of coalition building. But he also recognized, as did Madison before him, that this could be done only if one appealed to human reason. Unfortunately, the factional reformers' commitment to "fair representation" is one that appears blind to the difference between representing passion and representing reason. This could well be a result of their decided preference for democratic means as opposed to democratic results.

As important as representation is, responsible leaders must never lose sight of the all-important distinction Madison makes at the end of *Federalist* 49: "But it is the reason of public alone that ought to controul and regulate the government. The passions ought to be controuled and regulated by the government." Nowhere in the factional reformers' literature is there even the mildest hint that the Democratic party should give preference to human reason over human passion.

Conclusion

Political Parties as Auxiliary Precautions

The origin of the American two-party system is almost universally attributed to the ideological conflicts that developed in the early stages of America's constitutional republic. The ideological differences that existed were, no doubt, a major cause of America's early party development. Far too many students of America's party development make the mistake of assuming that this major cause was the sole cause of America's emerging political parties. A second cause for the emergence of political parties was the development of the popular branches of government. This has been the most neglected aspect of America's party origins.

The Madisonian Republicans advanced an anti-royalist theme which made Congress the natural home for their beliefs. Some thirty years later when the Van Buren Democrats were waging their war against such things as internal improvements financed by the federal government, the presidency was the natural branch to wage this first war against the pork-barrel politics we rightfully associate with Congress. In both of these cases, the beliefs that were being advanced fit more naturally in one branch of government than in the other.

A third aspect of the founding of America's party system must be acknowledged. Again, the two stages of the founding present two vitally important lessons. The development of congressional parties in the 1790s was for the explicit purpose of improving the organizational structure of the government. The development of presidential parties in the 1820s was for the explicit purpose of improving the electoral structure of the government. Organizing the government and managing elections continue to be the primary tasks of political parties.

To argue that parties originated for one and only one reason is the kind of oversimplification that is the hallmark of the reformers' approach to parties. A comprehensive understanding of the founding of America's two-party system is necessary to understanding why the more simplistic perspectives of the reformers have fallen short. It is both difficult and dangerous to attempt to overhaul a political system (or any system for that matter) that is not fully understood. Reformers who do not fully understand the system they are attempting to reform cannot fully understand or anticipate the consequences of their reform efforts.

E. E. Schattschneider was probably correct when he called the American political system the most complex system in the world, but recognizing that a system is complex and understanding those complexities are two very different things. Schattschneider's short-selling of the Constitution revealed the limits of his understanding. James MacGregor Burns appeared to have a slightly better understanding of the necessary interrelationship between our constitutional system and our party system, but when he discussed the two competing systems, he failed to recognize that they were both products of the Madisonian mind—a mind that never abandoned the new science of politics.

Yet this science is never mentioned in any of the reform literature. It is for this reason, in part, that the reformers we have examined have done little more than raise doubts about the American constitutional and party systems. They appear not to understand the systems fully, which may be why they cannot fully appreciate them.

The American party system grew out of the rich soil of the American constitutional system. The workings and complexity of the former are a direct result of the workings and complexity of the latter. This is why our party system is every bit as complex and confusing as our constitutional system. A more complete understanding of both systems must begin with an understanding of the new science of politics, for this is the theoretical foundation upon which the two systems were erected. This theoretical foundation prescribed four of the leading characteristics of our political system: separation of powers, federalism, republican institutions, and a government of limited powers.

Reformers who find any of these four characteristics unacceptable must acknowledge their opposition to the most fundamental parts of the American political founding. To attempt to avoid this admission is to be dishonest with themselves and with their audience. On this count, the Progressives were probably the most honest and open. In addition to the party reforms they were advancing, they proposed a number of constitutional amendments.[1] The responsible reformers, especially those who appeared after the turn of the twentieth century, tried very hard to minimize any discussion of constitutional change. The commission reformers appeared totally blind to the fact that there might be some link between parties and the Constitution.

The reformist persuasion has contended that the constitutional system we enjoy is a major obstacle to democracy. As we have seen, all of the reform groups have desired a purer form of democracy than the one set up by the Constitution and the American two-party system; they have advocated a more centralized system that would play a far more active role in our daily lives. While they did not agree on the methods required to improve our representative system, they did agree that the founders' approach is vastly inadequate. The Progressives desired a clearer and simpler majoritarian government which, for them, meant more executive-centered. The responsible reformers desired a clearer and simpler majoritarian government, but theirs would be party-centered.

In contrast, the commission reformers advocated a system that would be more representative of minority interests. These "minoritarian" reformers were not satisfied with a government that did no more than protect certain rights; they wanted a representative system that was more group oriented and less individually based. Basically, their view of representation fell somewhere between the American founders' and Karl Marx's position. In this respect, the commission reformers were no different from other interest group theorists.

What united these reformers intellectually was their dissatisfaction with the founders' ideas about representation. This is why they focused as much attention as they did on political parties. The Progressives wanted to weaken political parties, the responsibles wanted to strengthen political parties, and the fickle commissioners were not sure whether parties should be weaker or stronger but they knew they needed to be transformed.

The most consistent change advocated by the party reformers is one that focuses greater party attention on policies and less attention on principles. Such a change of emphasis has a price, but it is a price to which none of our reformers paid much attention. Unfortunately, it seems that they did not avoid this topic to strengthen their case; it is more likely that they simply did not understand the importance of this shift in attention.

By making parties more policy-oriented, the reform spirit would strip our party system of one of its most fundamental characteristics. It has been the parties' ability to rise above petty policy debates and focus on more fundamental questions that has led to America's most sweeping political transformations. It was more than policy differences that produced the political transformations of 1800, 1824, 1860, and 1932. These were times when America's party system transformed our political universe. While our parties may not always provide the clearest of policy alternatives and while they may not always be the easiest vehicles for translating majority interests into governmental action and may not always provide a unified governing unit, our parties have facilitated some of the most radical and far-reaching reforms that have occurred within any stable political system in the history of the world.

To underestimate or, worse yet, ignore this historic function of political parties is to miss what has been their most important service to the American political system. To discuss political parties without addressing this particular characteristic of American parties is like trying to describe baseball without mentioning batters. The realigning function political parties have performed has been their single greatest contribution to American politics. These have also been the times when America has gone through its most sweeping constitutional transformations.

Nothing has altered our constitutional consternation more radically than watershed elections. These have been the moments of our greatest political debates and our greatest political awareness. To lose these periodic constitutional examinations is to lose those rare moments when we as a nation reexamined our constitutional soul. By focusing on political principles instead of mere policies, political parties have been the vehicle for accomplishing a task Machiavelli considered to be the most important to the survival of a republic. Machiavelli argued that republics need to be brought back to their "original principles" periodically. This is precisely what watershed elections have accomplished for our republic.

Machiavelli believed that this renewal had to be the result of either some great statesman or some excellent laws. America's party system has facilitated an alliance between the people and laws to provide the "intrinsic prudence" needed to accommodate these political renovations.

> And it is a truth clearer than light that, without such renovations, these bodies cannot continue to exist; and the means of renewing them is to bring them back to their original principles. For, as all religious republics and monarchies must have within themselves some goodness, by means of which they obtain their first growth and reputation, and as in the process of time this goodness becomes corrupted, it will of necessity destroy the body unless something intervenes to bring it back to its normal condition.[2]

Forcing such constitutional examinations has been the role of our greatest statesmen. It has been their political vision that has truly refined and enlarged the public's view.

The Progressives were correct when they argued that bureaucrats could provide leadership, but they, like Burns, underestimated the towering genius that is required to present the entire nation with a renewed sense of purpose and a renewed understanding of the nation's mission. The facilitation of policy debates will not perform the same function for our nation.

Policy debates can take place between and among factions as easily as they do between and among political parties, but policy debates among factions are debates guided by the narrow understandings of their particular interests. Policy debates among political parties should be guided by an understanding of the political principles that are linked to our national interests.

The distinction between policy and principle is not always readily apparent to the great masses of American citizens. Statesmen attempt to clarify this important distinction; leaders frequently find that it serves their immediate needs to avoid this distinction. By directing political parties more toward the policy arena, reformers make it harder for parties to rise above the immediate concerns of the day; this, in turn, makes our political parties function more like the factions they were intended to transcend. The American party system emerged when we learned to distinguish between factions and parties; it will die when we lose sight of that distinction.

Herbert Croly argued that the post-Civil War Republicans were the first to use popular opinion to affront constitutional law. He further argued that the early Republicans were responsible for the shift from a Constitution that protected basic economic and property rights to a government that actively advanced economic opportunities. For him, this was the major breakthrough toward overcoming the limitations of a "monarchy of Law." This was America's first step toward a true democracy; at this point the will of the people took precedence over the rule of the Law.

The shift from a political system that merely protected rights to one that openly advanced interests was the critical watershed in American government and society. All the reformers we have studied seemed to accept Croly's understanding of this shift in the American political system. All the reformers we have studied desired a shift in our governance system that would allow us to take full advantage of this shift in political emphasis. All these reformers wanted that shift in our governance system to be structured in a way that would serve their particular vision of democracy. And all these reformers failed to comprehend the delicate balance that has been maintained by the founders' system—the very system that permits both the majoritarian and the minoritarian reformers to feel hopeful about what results might come from a few minor changes to the existing system.

The stability of the system created by the founders is what permits the majoritarians and minoritarians to function side by side. The majoritarian reformers—both the progressive and the responsible varieties—will continue to show some sympathy for factional reformers, provided the latter group does not enjoy too much success. In many ways, all reformers have a common enemy in the established constitutional order. The American two-party system provides a secure and legitimate forum for their assaults on the constitutional system. Disgruntled reformers have and will continue to have a natural home within the political party that is out of power.

Should one of these reform groups ever savor a full and complete victory within our political system, that group would not be as accommodating of its foes as is our current system. After all, it is the accommodating quality of our current constitutional system that reformers find so irksome. Both progressive and responsible reformers have called for the majority will to be a more dominant force in American politics. Nevertheless, while they have professed concern for minority interests, they do not want to be forced to cut deals with those interests when formulating policy.

In like manner, factional reformers want greater accommodations, not just safeguards, for minority interests. They also have professed a desire for greater democracy, but it is a different kind of democracy from that advocated by the majoritarian reformers. Greater democracy for the factional reformers is clearly interest group democracy. Their democracy, as noted above, is one that places greater emphasis on groups than on individuals. This is why the reformers can use a common rhetoric to advance radically different causes.

But let us not be misled. These groups have more in common than just rhetoric. If Croly is correct in his historical assessment of post-Civil War America, then the reforms of the 1960s and 1970s were designed simply to accomplish for civil rights what the reforms of the 1880s and 1890s did for economic rights. Let us also remember that there was a strong and very negative backlash to the policies the government was advancing in the 1880s and 1890s.

The Populists, Mugwumps, and Progressives were all groups organized around opposition to these new governmental initiatives. The Progressives made a passionate and largely successful call for reshaping our government to protect the majority of Americans from its distorted preferential politics. The reforms called for were all designed to advance the will of the majority over the preferred minorities. Croly described the progressive program as one that "was primarily an attempt to do away with privilege rather than an attempt to make privilege socially useful."[3]

Early indications reveal that the factional reformers of the Democratic party are the victims of a similar political backlash. They may want to argue that the Democratic party's electoral failures in recent years are the result of any number of other factors, such as Republican money, deep-seated prejudices, and media bias. A far simpler answer is that history is repeating itself. The lesson may be that there are limits to how far democratic societies are willing to go to advance the interests of minorities over the interest of the majority. Richard Nixon's appeal to the "silent majority" did work. If the Democrats fail to learn this lesson they will continue to suffer the results of their ignorance.

The historical role of political parties, at least the successful ones, has been to extend the precarious legal balance the Constitution strikes between majority and minority interests to the political arena. Their task has been one of accommodating the will of the majority without trampling on the rights of the minorities. Thomas Jefferson captured the spirit of this task in his first inaugural address, when he argued:

> All, too, will bear in mind this sacred principle, that though the will of the majority is in all cases to prevail, that will, to be rightful, must be reasonable; that the minority possess their equal rights, which equal laws must protect, and to violate which would be oppression.

The role reason must play in democratic government seems to be a lesson every generation must learn anew. Croly, Theodore Roosevelt, Woodrow Wilson, Schattschneider, and many others advocated the removal of the legal foundations of separation of powers in the name of responsibility or democracy, but this would do more than enhance the likelihood of majority rule. It would also free us from institutional safeguards which have impeded factional excesses. Gerald Pomper summarized the results of some of the most successful reforms, when he observed: "Whatever the progressives' intentions, the effect has been not to build a democratic community but to build the increasingly isolated, fractured non-community that we see in the United States."[4]

The legal obstacles that are maligned for preventing pure democracy are also the "inventions of prudence" that have given human reason a fighting chance to prevail over human passion. The founders were correct when they asserted that human reason will never guide a community that does not hold human passion in check. The passage of time has not altered this truth.

When the democratic spirit is freed from the "auxiliary precautions" the founders so carefully wove into the fabric of our government, political passions will gain the upper hand. Just as the majority spirit is emancipated from the shackles of legal safeguards, so are the multitudinous minority spirits. In this respect, the factional reformers were the heirs to the progressive reformers. Quite possibly, the responsible reformers could be as well, but the liberated democratic spirit is more naturally drawn to the fragmented politics of interest groups than to the more orderly politics of responsible rule. If it were not, democracies would have always had a natural remedy to the violence of faction, and the old science of politics would still reign supreme.

But this is not the case. The old science of politics was displaced by the new science of politics. The American contribution to this new science, the extended sphere, tipped the scales even more to the advantage of factional politics. The distinct geographical regions found it harder to understand the common bond they shared with their political brethren. Thus, the other contributions to the new science, like separation of powers, were made more, not less, necessary by the enlarged political orbit. As time has passed, the size of our republic has grown even larger, making those auxiliary precautions even more necessary.

But size was not the only factor that made the founders prefer a republican government to a democratic one. The much cited discussion of factions found in *Federalist* 10 was an introduction to that paper's final topic: the superiority of republics to democracies. Twentieth-century reformers are right when they argue that the founders were no friends of democracy. But they are wrong when they suggest that the founders were not friends of popular government. The dominant shortcoming of democracies prior to the eighteenth century was their instability. They were too often destroyed by their own excesses.

The democracies of antiquity had been convulsed internally by demagogues and factional splits; they had been overrun externally by more powerful and authoritarian states. Democracies were frail and turbulent states which had justly earned their bad reputation. The new science of politics was an effort to restore popular rule as a viable and responsible method of governance. The U.S. Constitution was the first serious effort to implement a popular government based on these new political principles.

Croly and other reformers may feel that we have outlived the need for such institutional safeguards, but their arguments do much to reveal their own lack of understanding. The key to the founders' success was their study of and commitment to a particular theory of government. The regime they established was firmly based on theoretical teachings that had been developed over centuries. Their work was not a tract for the times. History provided the opportunity; the founders produced a timeless political system firmly rooted in a realistic understanding of human nature.

Reformers who argue that the Constitution was an eighteenth-century document written for an eighteenth-century world are the ones who have misread the historical lesson of the past two centuries. Numerous changes have occurred in the political landscape during that time, and the Constitution's ability to adapt to these changes only confirms the wisdom of the founders' scheme.

One of the most significant changes that has occurred since the Constitution was ratified in 1789 was the development of our two-party system. Reformers like Wilson and Schattschneider have argued that parties' development uncovers one of the many miscalculations the founders made when they set up our political system. They could not be more wrong.

Quite the contrary, political parties lend further support to the founders' wisdom. After all, it was James Madison, author of *Federalist* 10, who actively developed our first national political party. This was not, as we noted earlier, due to any great intellectual or political metamorphosis. Reformers have consistently failed to see or understand the true lesson in Madison's political life.

First, Madison argued that factions were and always would be a part of any society that did not stifle basic liberty. He accepted factions as a permanent fixture in America. Nothing in his writings or speeches ever contradicted this position. Second, his argument in *Federalist* 10 was that the constitutional system he was advocating would control the violence of faction. The factions that were such a threat to America under the Articles of Confederation would pose less of a threat under the Constitution. With the ratification of the Constitution, Madison's concern over factions was mitigated. Furthermore, the party system he helped create in the 1790s did not fit the description he gave of factions in *The Federalist*.

Formal political parties organized around a clearly stated set of political principles which were developed to strengthen and defend our constitutional system are not what Madison was warning against. As we observed earlier, this was not a description of the political parties that developed in the 1790s, nor was it a description of any of the national parties that have emerged since that time. Madison's definition of a faction obviously applies to what we call interest groups today. The parties or factions that were assailed during the founding period had nothing in common with the national parties based on political principles that developed during the next decade. They resemble more closely the factious groups that have taken over the Democratic party's nominating conventions in recent years.

The factional reformers pose a different break from our constitutional system. In addition to encouraging the mischief of faction, they also would alter the nature of the presidential majority. The tremendous failure their reforms have met with at the ballot box cannot be denied. As we have noted, their efforts to adjust these reforms have been half-hearted, at best. The creation of superdelegates has done more to highlight the problem than to solve it.

As long as the Democrats steadfastly adhere to a fundamentally flawed theoretical policy, their fate is sealed. Jimmy Carter was elected at the peak of their electoral folly. Carter's election was a wonderful exception that clearly proved the rule. The majority coalition he forged was not entirely his own doing. The election of Bill Clinton in 1992 could signal a significant change in the Democratic party's presidential fate. But this will depend on his willingness and ability to move his party in the directions advocated by such moderate groups as the Democratic Leadership Council. If Clinton cannot reverse some of the mistakes the Democrats institutionalized between 1968 and 1988, his election will prove no more beneficial to his party than was Carter's.

The Watergate scandal, which forced the first presidential resignation in our history, took a heavy toll on the Republican party. The Republican party suffered severe losses in the 1974 off-year election; the Democrats emerged from that election with a two-thirds majority in both houses of Congress. By the mid–1970s, more American voters identified themselves as independents than as Republicans. Despite these advantages, Carter barely defeated his Republican rival, Gerald Ford.

Carter's election gave the Democrats decisive control of all the popular branches in the federal government. Their inability to capitalize on this opportunity was caused by a number of factors, most important among these being the crippling effect of the Democratic nominating process. The nominating process that resulted from the factional reforms assured a hostile relationship between the president and Congress. The interest groups represented at the Democratic convention were incompatible with the geographical groups represented in Congress. The old nominating process utilized our federal system to build a presidential majority. When state parties controlled their own delegate selection process, the national convention was a composite of the majorities within the existing states. As such, the convention delegates reflected the kinds of majorities that the president would be working with on Capitol Hill and in the state capitols.

Clinton arrived in Washington with better ties to both Capitol Hill and the state capitols than had Carter; the extent of his effectiveness should provide further insights into the full impact of the Democratic party's reforms. If Clinton is successful in his dealings with Congress, it will be in spite of, not because of, the Democratic party's nominating process.

Under the old system, the presidential nominating process tested a candidate's ability to work with and lead other elected officials. The old nominating system encouraged cooperation with other elected officials, the kind of cooperation needed to govern effectively. Presidential nominating conventions were created to build party ties and strengthen the federal aspects of the party system. This last point is one that all party reformers have failed to appreciate.

The federal aspect of our two-party system is ignored at great peril. Party nominating conventions were developed to replace the old King Caucus in order to broaden the party's political base. This base was broadened by making presidential nominations less national and more federal in scope, which made sound political sense because the Electoral College has strong federal characteristics. Although most reformers have expressed dissatisfaction with the Electoral College, it is still the constitutional method we use to elect our chief executive.

All the reformers we have studied harbor disdain for the federal characteristics of our political system. But this aspect of our political system is one more example of the founders' good sense and judgment. It is the federal characteristic of our system that has been most imitated by other republics. The enlarged orbit of American government, which made federalism necessary, was designed to increase the number of factions so no one group would make a majority. This, more than anything else, made political parties a necessary component of the American political system.

The political successes of Thomas Jefferson, Andrew Jackson, and Abraham Lincoln took place within the traditional two-party system. These presidents used the party system to bring about significant changes—changes that were stimulated by lively debate about the nature of our political system and the proper interpretation of our constitutional system. The balance between the two popular branches of government, as well as between the state and national levels of government, was at the heart of those historical debates.

The Constitution, with the aid of our two-party system, has permitted the refinement and enlargement of the public's view. It is this refinement that has created reasonable majorities. If either the progressive or the responsible reformers achieve the upper hand, the majority party will be less inclined toward reasonable justifications for their actions, and the rights of minorities will suffer; if the factional reformers prevail, no reasonable justification will be needed because no discernible majority interest will ever prevail.

A party system that is truly compatible with the constitutional system is one that encourages the politics of elections to forge the same kind of coalition that will be needed to govern. When practitioners as well as scholars fail to understand this most fundamental aspect of our political system there is no reason to expect the average voter to realize it. No wonder there continues to be such confusion surrounding America's two-party system.

Notes

Introduction (pages 1 to 11)

1. Joseph Charles, *The Origins of the American Party System* (New York: Harper & Row, 1956), p. 6.

2. John Chester Miller, *The Federalist Era, 1789–1809* (New York: Harper, 1963), p. 103.

3. *Origins of the American Party System*, p. 80. Charles develops this argument in considerable detail in pp. 74–90.

4. *The Federalist Era*, p. 102.

5. *The Papers of James Madison*, edited by Robert A. Rutland et al. (Charlottesville: University Press of Virginia, 1983), Vol. 14, p. 370.

6. Lincoln's observations indicate that passion plays an important role in the founding of a regime but that reason is crucial to maintaining a regime. Martin Diamond reverses the roles of reason and passion in his discussion of this topic found in "The Federalist," in Morton Frisch and Richard Stevens, editors, *American Political Thought* (New York: Scribner's, 1971), p. 68.

7. "A Candid State of Parties," *National Gazette*, September 22, 1792. All references to Madison's party essays are taken from *The Papers of James Madison*, edited by Rutland et al., vol. 14.

8. *Papers of James Madison*, 14:372.

9. The works that address Madison's party essays are Marvin Meyers, *Mind of the Founder* (Hanover, N.H.: University Press of New England, 1981); Edward S. Dreyer, "Making Parties Respectable: James Madison's National Gazette Essays," paper presented at the American Political Science Association Convention in 1987; and Colleen Sheehan, "Madison's Party Press Essays," in *Interpretation* (Spring 1990).

10. *Papers of James Madison*, 14:157–69.

11. *Papers of James Madison*, 14:158–59.

12. *Papers of James Madison*, 14:159.

13. *Papers of James Madison*, 14:167.

14. Sheehan, "Madison's Party Press Essays," p. 355.

15. John Zvesper provides a good summary of different assumptions on this

113

topic in *Political Philosophy and Rhetoric: A Study of the Origins of American Party Politics* (Cambridge: Cambridge University Press, 1977), pp. 10–16.

16. *Papers of James Madison*, 14:372.

17. The most interesting letters during this period are those Madison sent to and received from George Nicholas and John Beckley.

18. Two examples of this criticism range from Zvesper's mild statement in *Political Philosophy and Rhetoric*, pp. 113–14, to Edward McNall Burns's harsher assessment in *James Madison: Philosopher of the Constitution* (New Brunswick, N.J.: Rutgers University Press, 1938), p. 200.

19. Adrienne Koch provides a different, but no less sympathetic, interpretation of these "inconsistencies" in *Madison's "Advice To My Country"* (Princeton: Princeton University Press, 1966), pp. 116–19.

20. For a detailed discussion of this issue see my essay titled "From Factions to Parties: America's Partisan Education" in Thomas Silver and Peter Schramm, editors, *Natural Right and Political Right: Essays in Honor of Harry V. Jaffa* (Durham: Carolina Academic Press, 1984).

21. Richard Hofstadter, *The Idea of a Party System* and Robert Remini, *Martin Van Buren and the Democratic Party* (New York: Columbia University Press, 1959) are the best-known works that discuss the importance of Van Buren's contribution. I find James Ceaser's discussion of Van Buren in *Presidential Selection: Theory and Development* (Princeton: Princeton University Press, 1979) to be the most helpful secondary work available. Like Ceaser, I believe party development was a "deliberate" act and that it was intended "to prevent presidential elections from being decided in the House . . ." (p. 123). This last point is more central to my thesis. Van Buren was as committed to freeing the presidency from congressional influence during the nominating process as he was to reducing its likely involvement during the final selection.

22. The most organized and systematic group of progressive reformers has been the Democratic Leadership Council (DLC) and its companion organization the Progressive Policy Institute. Bill Clinton was the head of the DLC for a time and used that position to develop his national political base. Al From, executive director of the DLC, was a member of Clinton's transition team. During its 1993 annual conference, the DLC gave the Clinton administration mixed reviews.

23. George W. Carey, "The Separation of Powers," in George J. Graham Jr. and Scarlett G. Graham, editors, *Founding Principles of American Government: Two Hundred Years of Democracy on Trial* (Bloomington: Indiana University Press, 1977), p. 98.

24. Harvey C. Mansfield Jr., *America's Constitutional Soul* (Baltimore: Johns Hopkins University Press, 1991), p. 122. This entire chapter, "Separation of Powers in the American Constitution," is one of the best short statements on the virtues of separation of powers available. Two other helpful works on this topic are George W. Carey, *The Federalist* (Urbana: University of Illinois Press, 1989), especially Chapter 2, and David F. Epstein, *The Political Theory of The Federalist* (Chicago: University of Chicago Press, 1984), especially Chapter 5.

Chapter One (pages 13 to 26)

1. Samuel Duncan-Clark, *The Progressive Movement: Its Principles and Its Programme* (Boston: Small, Maynard, 1913), p. xiv.
2. *The New Republic*, August 21, 1915, p. 60.
3. *Progressive Movement*, pp. 56–57.
4. *Progressive Movement*, pp. 57–58.
5. "Purpose and Policies of the Progressive Party," speech delivered before the Progressive Party Convention, August 6, 1912.
6. *Progressive Movement*, p. 47.
7. Theodore Roosevelt, *Social Justice and Popular Rule* (New York: Scribner's, 1925), p. 58.
8. Harry V. Jaffa, *Equality and Liberty: Theory and Practice in American Politics* (Oxford: Oxford University Press, 1965), pp. 39–40.
9. Harry V. Jaffa, *Crisis of the House Divided* (New York: Doubleday, 1959), pp. 198–99.
10. *The New Republic*, November 14, 1914, p. 11.
11. Herbert Croly, *Progressive Democracy* (New York: Macmillan, 1914), pp. 10–11.
12. *Progressive Democracy*, p. 343.
13. *Presidential Selection*, p. 158. Ceaser argued that the development of national conventions coupled with the demise of the founding generation were important elements in shaping the new kind of leadership our nation would experience: "By admitting partisanship in the form of a coalitional party into the selection process, it could be said the presidency was being pulled down from its pedestal of independence above the contending factions."
14. *Progressive Democracy*, p. 311.
15. *Progressive Democracy*, p. 313.
16. *Progressive Democracy*, p. 361.
17. *Progressive Democracy*, p. 168.
18. *Progressive Democracy*, p. 200.
19. *Progressive Democracy*, p. 208.
20. *Progressive Democracy*, p. 427.
21. *Progressive Democracy*, p. 173.
22. *Progressive Democracy*, pp. 177–78.
23. Robert La Follette, *Autobiography* (Madison: La Follette, 1913), p. 104.
24. David Thelen, "Two Traditions of Progressive Reform, Political Parties and American Democracy" in Patricia Bonomi et al. editors, *The American Constitutional System Under Strong and Weak Parties*, (New York: Praeger, 1981), p. 41.
25. Thelen, p. 37.
26. John Chamberlain, *Farewell to Reform: The Rise, Life and Decay of the Progressive Mind in America* (Chicago: Quadrangle Books, 1932, 1965), p. 155.
27. *The Collected Works of Abraham Lincoln*, Roy Basler, editor (New Brunswick, N.J.: Rutgers University Press, 1953), III:455.

Chapter Two (pages 27 to 42)

1. One of the better discussions of this system can be found in Ceaser, *Presidential Selection*, Chapter V. Woodrow Wilson acknowledged and endorsed this shift in presidential leadership in *Constitutional Government* (New York: Columbia University Press, 1908). This work is reprinted in *The Papers of Woodrow Wilson*, Arthur Link, editor (Princeton: Princeton University Press, 1966), XVIII: 69–216. The academic tone of Wilson's book presents the topic in a more descriptive manner. His main thesis was that we need to think of the Constitution in terms of Darwinian theory rather than Newtonian theory. He described the shifting role of the president and political parties as major forces in our evolving political system, but was less decisive than Roosevelt in making this a political cause.

2. Theodore Roosevelt, *Social Justice and Popular Rule* (New York: Scribner's, 1925; reprinted New York: Arno Press, 1974), pp. 179–80.

3. Numerous works develop the setting and circumstances that led to the reforms of this era. Croly's *The Promise of American Life* (New York: Macmillan, 1909) and La Follette's *Autobiography* are two passionate statements from that period. Richard L. McCormick, *The Party Period and Public Policy: American Politics from the Age of Jackson to the Progressive Era* (Oxford: Oxford University Press, 1986), Chapters 6 to 9, is especially helpful concerning the issues and events of this period. Two other works that cover this period and events are Lewis L. Gould, editor, *The Progressive Era* (Syracuse: Syracuse University Press, 1974), and Richard Hofstadter, *The Age of Reform: From Bryan to F.D.R.* (New York: Knopf, 1955).

4. *Presidential Addresses and State Papers of Theodore Roosevelt* (New York: Collier, 1970), I:472. Hereafter referred to as *Presidential Addresses*. It is interesting to compare the statement Roosevelt made here with the position Jefferson took in Query XIX of his *Notes on the State of Virginia*.

5. *Crisis of the House Divided*, p. 327.

6. *Crisis of the House Divided*, p. 327.

7. *Social Justice and Popular Rule: Essays, Addresses, and Public Statements Relating to the Progressive Movement (1910–1916)* (New York: Arno Press, 1974), pp. 148–49. Hereafter referred to as *Social Justice*.

8. *Social Justice*, pp. 149–50.

9. *Social Justice*, p. 145.

10. *Social Justice*, p. 239.

11. *Social Justice*, p. 27.

12. Theodore Roosevelt, *Theodore Roosevelt: An Autobiography* (New York: Scribner's, 1924), pp. 362–65.

13. *Social Justice*, p. 146.

14. *Social Justice*, p. 146.

15. *Social Justice*, p. 317.

16. *Social Justice*, p. 145.

17. *Social Justice*, pp. 163–97. All quotations in this section will be from this address unless otherwise noted.

18. *Social Justice*, p. 137.
19. *Social Justice*, pp. 116–17. This same point is developed more fully in a speech appropriately titled "The Recall of Judicial Decisions," found on pp. 255–71 of the same volume.
20. *Presidential Addresses*, III-IV:374.
21. Most constitutional law and history books provide a detailed description of the different jurisprudential schools. One of the better descriptions is in Alfred H. Kelly, Winfred A. Harbison, and Herman Belz, *The American Constitution: Its Origins and Development*, 6th ed. (New York: Norton, 1983), pp. 466–67. Sociological jurisprudence is an interpretive school closely associated with the progressive movement.
22. *Social Justice*, pp. 128–29.
23. *Presidential Addresses*, III-IV:365.
24. *Social Justice*, p. 203.
25. *Presidential Addresses*, I-II:191.
26. Joseph Bucklin Bishop, *Theodore Roosevelt and His Time: Shown in His Own Letters* (New York: Scribner's, 1920), II:354.
27. *Theodore Roosevelt and His Time*, II:354.
28. *Progressive Movement*, p. 110.
29. *Promise of American Life*, p. 283.
30. *Promise of American Life*, p. 284.
31. Cited in Charles Merriam and Harold Gosnell, *The American Party System* (New York: Macmillan, 1930), pp. 43–44.
32. Nelson Polsby discussed the problems such a shift can create in *Consequences of Party Reform* (Oxford: Oxford University Press, 1983), p. 66.
33. Harvey Mansfield, Jr., *Taming the Prince* (New York: Free Press, 1989), p. 256.

Chapter Three (pages 43 to 55)

1. Woodrow Wilson, *The Papers of Woodrow Wilson*, Arthur Link, editor (Princeton: Princeton University Press, 1966), I:498. Hereafter referred to as *Papers*.
2. "Government by Debate," *Papers*, II:206.
3. "Government by Debate," *Papers*, II:230.
4. "Government by Debate," *Papers*, II:231.
5. "Government by Debate," *Papers*, II:232.
6. "Cabinet Government," *Papers*, I:507.
7. "Government by Debate," *Papers*, II:162.
8. "Government by Debate," *Papers*, II:167.
9. "Cabinet Government," *Papers*, I:496.
10. "Cabinet Government," *Papers*, I:494.
11. "Cabinet Government," *Papers*, I:495.

12. "Cabinet Government," *Papers*, I:494.

13. "Government by Debate," *Papers*, II:200.

14. "Cabinet Government," *Papers*, I:502.

15. Woodrow Wilson, *Congressional Government* (Cleveland: World, 1885; reprinted Gloucester, Mass.: Smith, 1973), pp. 142–43.

16. *Constitutional Government*, in *Papers*, XVIII:105. By 1908 Wilson seems to have abandoned his desire for amending the Constitution to create a cabinet system. This is probably because he has a clearer vision of how much potential the president has in reshaping the political system. Roosevelt's years in the White House may have revealed just how much could be accomplished by a strong and active president. A careful reading of *Congressional Government* and *Constitutional Government* reveals considerable consistency in what Wilson considers to be the problem confronting our political system; however, his solution to that problem shifts from the Constitution and Congress in his earlier work to political parties and the president in the latter.

17. "Government by Debate," *Papers*, II:167.

18. "Government by Debate," *Papers*, II:168.

19. "Government by Debate," *Papers*, II:168.

20. *Congressional Government*, p. 172.

21. *Congressional Government*, p. 171. Wilson discussed this matter in a comparative perspective on pp. 167–68.

22. "Government by Debate," *Papers*, II:227. This was one of the suggestions that made this essay "too radical" for publication. Letter from Robert Bridges, February 2, 1883. *Papers*, II:296–97.

23. "Government by Debate," *Papers*, II:247. *Congressional Government*, p. 127.

24. *Congressional Government*, p. 168.

25. *Congressional Government*, p. 166.

26. *Congressional Government*, p. 173.

27. "Government by Debate," *Papers*, II:184.

28. "Cabinet Government," *Papers*, I:505.

29. "Cabinet Government," *Papers*, I:506.

30. "Government by Debate," *Papers*, II:240.

31. *Congressional Government*, p. 27.

32. *Congressional Government*, p. 28.

33. "Government by Debate," *Papers*, II:202.

34. "Cabinet Government," *Papers*, I:499. He discussed the need for these changes in "Government by Debate," *Papers*, II:202–3 and *Congressional Government*, pp. 167–68.

35. "Government by Debate," *Papers*, II:202.

36. "Cabinet Government," *Papers*, I:509.

37. See Lippman's introduction to *Congressional Government*, pp. 11–12.

38. Austin Ranney, *The Doctrine of Responsible Party Government* (Urbana: University of Illinois Press, 1962), pp. 28–29.

39. "Cabinet Government," *Papers*, I:504.

40. While this position has already been noted, it is developed more fully in Wilson's "The Study of Administration," *Political Science Quarterly*, June 1887.

Chapter Four (pages 57 to 72)

1. E. E. Schattschneider, *Party Government* (New York: Rinehart, 1942), p. 4.

2. *Party Government*, p. 8.

3. *Party Government*, p. 9.

4. *Party Government*, p. 2.

5. *Party Government*, p. 7.

6. This distinction between factions and parties has puzzled many political analysts over the years. There was a similar problem with the term *federalism*. What that term meant in 1788 was quite different from what it has meant since the turn of the twentieth century. Most scholars understand that the meaning of the term *Federal* has altered because of the American constitutional system. The term *party* has witnessed a similar transformation but this change seems harder for many respected students of politics to comprehend. Austin Ranney perpetuated this misunderstanding in a curious manner in *Curing the Mischief of Faction: Party Reform in America* (Berkeley and Los Angeles: University of California Press, 1975), Chapter 2. One of the clearest statements on the founders' understanding of parties is Harry V. Jaffa's discussion in "The Nature and Origin of the American Party System," in Robert A. Goldwin, editor, *Political Parties, U.S.A.* (Chicago: Rand McNally, 1961).

7. *Papers of James Madison*, 14:217.

8. "Toward a More Responsible Two-Party System: A Report of the Committee on Political Parties, American Political Science Association," *American Political Science Review* (September 1950, supplement):1. Hereafter referred to as "More Responsible."

9. *Party Government*, p. 124.

10. *Party Government*, p. 124.

11. *Party Government*, p. 126.

12. James MacGregor Burns, *The Deadlock of Democracy: Four-Party Politics in America* (Englewood Cliffs, N.J.: Prentice-Hall, 1963), p. 22.

13. This point is made especially clear by Kenneth M. Dolbeare and Linda Metcalf in "The Dark Side of the Constitution" in John F. Manley and Kenneth M. Dolbeare, editors, *The Case Against the Constitution* (Armonk: Sharpe, 1987).

14. The most detailed examination of the early responsible advocates is Ranney, *Doctrine of Responsible Party Government*. A good survey of the more recent literature is Leon Epstein's Presidential Address to the American Political Science Association titled "What Happened to the British Party Model?" in *American Political Science Review* (March 1980).

15. *Party Government*, pp. 2, 53.

16. *Party Government*, pp. 206–7.

17. *Party Government*, p. 208.

18. *Party Government*, p. 209.

19. *Party Government*, p. 210.

20. My criticism of the report's style is mild compared to the criticism made by committee member Evron Kirkpatrick. His criticism of the style as well as the substance of the report is clearly detailed in his article "Toward a More Responsible Two-Party System: Political Science, Policy Science, or Pseudo-Science?" *American Political Science Review* (December 1971), pp. 965–90. This work also has one of the most comprehensive bibliographies on the secondary literature on this report.

21. "More Responsible," p. 1.

22. "More Responsible," p. 4.

23. "More Responsible," p. 5.

24. "More Responsible," p. 36.

25. "More Responsible," p. 58.

26. "More Responsible," p. 5.

27. "More Responsible," pp. 6, 7, 10, 39–44, 67–69.

28. "More Responsible," p. 23.

29. *Deadlock of Democracy*, pp. 326–27.

30. *Deadlock of Democracy*, p. 340. Burns has been remarkably consistent on this notion. Leadership has continued to be a central theme in his writings and political parties have continued to be a major vehicle through which that leadership could and should be channeled. Burns's other books on this general topic are *Leadership* (New York: Harper & Row, 1978) and *The Power to Lead* (New York: Simon & Schuster, 1984). Unfortunately both Burns and Wilson want leadership to have an institutional anchor or base. There appears to be a subtle yet important distinction between the political leadership advocated by many reformers and the notion of statesmanship described by Lincoln in his speech on the "Perpetuation of Our Political Institutions," delivered to the Young Men's Lyceum in 1838. For a detailed discussion of statesmanship see Paul Eidelberg, *A Discourse on Statesmanship* (Urbana: University of Illinois Press, 1974).

31. This list of "specific elements" is found in Chapter 14: "Strategy for Americans."

32. "More Responsible," p. 20.

33. *Deadlock of Democracy*, p. 332.

Chapter Five (pages 73 to 85)

1. "Second Report of the Special Equal Rights Committee" (Washington, D.C.: Democratic National Committee, 1968), p. 3.

2. McGovern-Fraser Commission Report, *Mandate for Reform: Report of the Commission on Party Structure and Delegate Selection to the Democratic Na-*

tional Committee (Washington, D.C.: Democratic National Committee, 1970), p. 14. Hereafter referred to as *Mandate*.

3. Hughes Commission Report, *The Democratic Choice: Report of the Commission on the Democratic Selection of Presidential Nominees* (Washington, D.C.: Democratic National Committee, 1968), p. 1. Hereafter referred to as *Democratic Choice*.

4. *New York Times*, January 19, 1968.

5. *Democratic Choice*, p. 2.

6. *Democratic Choice*, p. 13.

7. *Democratic Choice*, pp. 13–14.

8. *Democratic Choice*, p. 14.

9. *Democratic Choice*, p. 34.

10. *Democratic Choice*, p. 34.

11. *Democratic Choice*, pp. 34–35.

12. *Mandate*, p. 15.

13. *Mandate*, p. 14.

14. James MacGregor Burns listed such "consolidation" as the parties' first objective for developing real two-party competition; *Deadlock of Democracy*, pp. 327–28.

15. James Ceaser and Andrew Busch, *Upside Down and Inside Out: The 1992 Elections and American Politics* (Savage, Md.: Rowman & Littlefield, 1993), pp. 164–66.

16. Theodore Lowi and Benjamin Ginsberg, *Democrats Return to Power: Politics and Policy in the Clinton Era* (New York and London: Norton, Inc., 1994). This short work does not paint a very optimistic picture for the Clinton administration.

17. *Consequences of Party Reform*, p. 65. Larry Sabato developed this same point when he made a case for political parties in *The Party's Just Begun: Shaping Political Parties for America's Future* (Boston: Scott, Foresman, 1988); see especially Chapter 1.

18. Winograd Commission Report, *Openness, Participation and Party Building: Reforms to a Stronger Democratic Party* (Washington, D.C.: Democratic National Committee, 1978), p. 7.

19. *National Journal*, January 2, 1982, p. 27.

20. *Presidential Selection*, p. 263, note 3. Sabato claims that much of the increase in primaries in recent years has been a result of popular demand; *Party's Just Begun*, pp. 206–8.

21. Byron Shafer, *Quiet Revolution: The Struggle for the Democratic Party and the Shaping of Post-Reform Politics* (New York: Russell Sage, 1983), p. 202.

22. Milburn L. Wilson, *Democracy Has Roots* (New York: Carrick & Evans, 1939), p. 92.

Chapter Six (pages 87 to 98)

1. *Origins of the American Party System*, pp. 83–85.

2. *Party Period and Public Policy*, p. 161.

3. Alexis de Tocqueville, *Democracy in America*, edited by Phillip Bradley, 2 vols. (New York: Random House, 1945), 1:185.

4. *Democracy in America*, 1:182.

5. *National Journal*, August 23, 1980, p. 1388.

6. *National Journal*, August 23, 1980, p. 1388.

7. Hunt Commission, *A Time of Renewal: Report of the Commission on Presidential Nomination* (Washington, D.C.: Democratic National Committee, 1982), pp. 1–2. This commission was chaired by Governor James B. Hunt Jr. of North Carolina. Hereafter referred to as *Time for Renewal*.

8. *Time for Renewal*, p. 2.

9. *Time for Renewal*, p. 6.

10. *Congressional Quarterly*, January 23, 1982, p. 127.

11. *Time for Renewal*, p. 11.

12. *Time for Renewal*, p. 8.

13. *Time for Renewal*, p. 9.

14. *Time for Renewal*, pp. 9–10.

15. *Time for Renewal*, p. 8.

16. *Time for Renewal*, p. 15.

17. *Time for Renewal*, p. 16.

18. *Openness, Participation, and Party Building*, pp. 10–15.

19. *Time for Renewal*, pp. 10–11.

20. *Mandate*, p. 40.

21. *Quiet Revolution*, pp. 206–7 and Chapter 17.

22. *Time for Renewal*, Rules 4–6.

23. *Time for Renewal*, p. 14.

24. *Time for Renewal*, p. 2.

25. *Delegate Selection Rules for the 1988 Democratic National Convention* (Washington, D.C.: Democratic National Committee, no date), p. 5.

26. Walter Berns, *Taking the Constitution Seriously* (Lanham, Md.: University Press of America, 1991), pp. 178–83.

Conclusion (pages 99 to 109)

1. The Sixteenth through the Nineteenth Amendments are the ones that were a result of the progressive movement.

2. Niccolò Machiavelli, *The Discourses* (New York: Random House, 1950).

3. *Progressive Democracy*, pp. 107–8.

4. *The American Constitutional System Under Strong and Weak Parties*, p. 66.

Bibliography

Books

Beard, Charles. *An Economic Interpretation of the Constitution of the United States.* New York: Macmillan, 1913.

Berns, Walter. *Taking the Constitution Seriously.* Lanham, Md.: University Press of America, 1991.

Bishop, Joseph Bucklin. *Theodore Roosevelt and His Time: Shown in His Own Letters.* New York: Scribner's, 1920.

Bonomi, Patricia; Burns, James M.; and Ranney, Austin, eds. *The American Constitutional System Under Strong and Weak Parties.* New York: Praeger, 1981.

Burns, Edward McNall. *James Madison: Philosopher of the Constitution.* New Brunswick: Rutgers University Press, 1938.

Burns, James MacGregor. *The Deadlock of Democracy.* Englewood Cliffs, N.J.: Prentice-Hall, 1963.

————. *Leadership.* New York: Harper & Row, 1978.

————. *The Power to Lead.* New York: Simon & Schuster, 1984.

Carey, George W. *The Federalist.* Urbana: University of Illinois Press, 1989.

Ceaser, James. *Presidential Selection: Theory and Development.* Princeton: Princeton University Press, 1979.

Ceaser, James, and Busch, Andrew. *Upside Down and Inside Out: The 1992 Elections and American Politics.* Savage, Md.: Rowman & Littlefield, 1993.

Chamberlain, John. *Farewell to Reform: The Rise, Life and Decay of the Progressive Mind in America.* Chicago: Quadrangle Books, 1932; reprinted ed., 1965.

Charles, Joseph. *The Origin of the American Party System.* New York: Harper & Row, 1956.

Croly, Herbert. *Progressive Democracy.* New York: Macmillan, 1914.

————. *The Promise of American Life.* New York: Macmillan, 1909; reprinted ed., Cambridge: Belknap Press, 1965.

Duncan-Clark, Samuel. *The Progressive Movement: Its Principles and Its Programme.* Boston: Small, Maynard, 1913.

Eidelberg, Paul. *A Discourse on Statesmanship.* Urbana: University of Illinois, 1974.

123

Epstein, David F. *The Political Theory of The Federalist.* Chicago: University of Chicago Press, 1984.

Frisch, Morton, and Stevens, Richard. *American Political Thought.* New York: Scribner's, 1971.

Goldwin, Robert, ed. *Political Parties, U.S.A.* Chicago: Rand McNally, 1961.

Gould, Lewis, ed. *The Progressive Era.* Syracuse: Syracuse University Press, 1974.

Graham, George J., and Graham, Scarlett G. *Founding Principles of the American Government: Two Hundred Years of Democracy on Trial.* Bloomington: Indiana University Press, 1977.

Hamilton, Alexander; Madison, James; and Jay, John. *The Federalist.* Edited by Jacob E. Cooke. Middletown, Conn.: Wesleyan University Press, 1961.

Hofstadter, Richard. *The Age of Reform: From Bryan to F.D.R.* New York: Knopf, 1955.

———. *The Idea of a Party System.* Berkeley: University of California Press, 1969.

Jaffa, Harry. *The Crisis of the House Divided: An Interpretation of the Issues in the Lincoln-Douglas Debates.* Garden City, N.Y.: Doubleday, 1959.

———. *Equality and Liberty: Theory and Practice in American Politics.* New York: Oxford University Press, 1965.

Jefferson, Thomas. *Notes on the State of Virginia.* New York: Harper & Row, 1964.

Kelly, Alfred H.; Harbison, Winfred A.; and Belz, Herman. *The American Constitution: Its Origins and Development.* 6th ed. New York: Norton, 1983.

Koch, Adrienne. *Madison's "Advice To My Nation."* Princeton: Princeton University Press, 1966.

La Follette, Robert. *Autobiography.* Madison: Robert M. La Follette Company, 1913.

Lincoln, Abraham. *The Collected Works of Abraham Lincoln.* Edited by Roy P. Basler. New Brunswick: Rutgers University Press, 1953.

Lowi, Theodore, and Ginsberg, Benjamin. *Democrats Return to Power.* New York: Norton, 1994.

Machiavelli, Niccolò. *The Prince and the Discourses.* Translated by Luigi Ricci. New York: Random House, 1950.

Madison, James. *The Mind of the Founder: Sources of the Political Thought of James Madison.* Edited by Marvin Meyers. Indianapolis and New York: Bobbs-Merrill, 1973.

———. *The Papers of James Madison.* Edited by Robert A. Rutland and Charles F. Hobson. Charlottesville: University Press of Virginia, 1977.

Mansfield, Harvey C. *America's Constitutional Soul.* Baltimore: Johns Hopkins University Press, 1991.

———. *Taming the Prince.* New York: Free Press, 1989.

Manley, Charles, and Dolbeare, Kenneth, eds. *The Case Against the Constitution: From the Antifederalist to the Present.* Armonk, N.Y.: Sharpe, 1987.

McCormick, Richard L. *The Party Period and Public Policy: American Politics from the Age of Jackson to the Progressive Era.* New York: Oxford University Press, 1986.

Merriam, Charles, and Gosnell, Harold. *The American Party System.* New York: Macmillan, 1930.

Miller, John Chester. *The Federalist Era, 1789–1809.* New York: Harper & Row, 1963.

Polsby, Nelson. *Consequences of Party Reform.* New York: Oxford University Press, 1983.

Ranney, Austin. *Curing the Mischief of Faction: Party Reform in America.* Berkeley: University of California Press, 1975.

————. *The Doctrine of Responsible Party Government.* Urbana: University of Illinois Press, 1962.

Remini, Robert. *Martin Van Buren and the Democratic Party.* New York: Columbia University Press, 1959.

Roosevelt, Theodore. *Presidential Addresses and State Papers of Theodore Roosevelt.* New York: Collier, 1970.

————. *Social Justice and Popular Rule: Essays, Addresses, and Public Statements Relating to the Progressive Movement (1910–1916).* New York: Scribner's, 1925; reprinted ed., New York: Arno Press, 1974.

————. *Theodore Roosevelt: An Autobiography.* New York: Scribner's, 1924.

Sabato, Larry. *The Party's Just Begun.* Boston: Scott, Foreman & Co., 1988.

Schattschneider, Elmer E. *Party Government.* New York: Rinehart, 1942.

Shafer, Byron. *Quiet Revolution: The Struggle for the Democratic Party and the Shaping of Post-Reform Politics.* New York: Russell Sage, 1983.

Silver, Thomas, and Schramm, Peter, eds. *Natural Right and Political Right: Essays in Honor of Harry V. Jaffa.* Durham: Carolina Academic Press, 1984.

Smith, J. Allen. *The Spirit of American Government.* Cambridge, Mass.: Harvard University Press, 1965.

Tocqueville, Alexis de. *Democracy in America.* Edited by Phillip Bradley. New York: Random House, 1945.

Van Buren, Martin. *Inquiry into The Origin and Course of Political Parties in the United States.* New York: Hurd & Houghton, 1867.

Wilson, Milburn L. *Democracy Has Roots.* New York: Carrick & Evans, 1939.

Wilson, Woodrow. *Congressional Government.* Cleveland: World, 1885; reprinted ed., Gloucester, Mass.: Peter Smith, 1973.

————. *Constitutional Government.* New York: Columbia University Press, 1908.

————. *The Papers of Woodrow Wilson.* Edited by Arthur Link. Princeton: Princeton University Press, 1966.

Zvesper, John. *Political Philosophy and Rhetoric: A Study of the Origins of American Party Politics.* Cambridge: Cambridge University Press, 1977.

Reports

The Democratic Choice: Report of the Commission on the Democratic Selection of Presidential Nominees. Harold E. Hughes, Chairman. Washington, D.C.: Democratic National Committee, 1968.

Democrats All: A Report of the Commission on Delegate Selection and Party Structure. Barbara A. Mikulski, Chairwoman. Washington, D.C.: Democratic National Committee, 1974.

Delegate Selection Rules for the 1988 Democratic National Convention. Washington, D.C.: Democratic National Committee, 1988.

Mandate for Reform: A Report of the Commission on Party Structure and Delegate Selection to the Democratic National Committee. George S. McGovern, Chairman. Washington, D.C.: Democratic National Committee, 1970.

Openness, Participation and Party Building: Reforms for a Stronger Democratic Party, Report of the Commission on Presidential Nomination and Party Structure. Morley A. Winograd, Chairman. Washington, D.C.: Democratic National Committee, 1978.

"Second Report of the Special Equal Rights Committee." Washington, D.C.: Democratic National Committee, 1968.

A Time of Renewal: Report of the Commission on Presidential Nominations. James B. Hunt, Chairman. Washington, D.C.: Democratic National Committee, 1982.

Articles and Papers

American Political Science Association. "Toward a More Responsible Two-Party System," Report of the Committee on Political Parties. *American Political Science Review*, Supplement vol. 44 (September 1950).

Dreyer, Edward S. "Making Parties Responsible: James Madison's National Gazette Essays." Paper presented at the American Political Association Convention, Chicago, September 7, 1987.

Epstein, Leon. "What Happened to the British Party Model?" *American Political Science Review* (March 1980).

"The Future of the Two-Party System." *The New Republic* (November 14, 1914).

Kirkpatrick, Evron. "Toward a More Responsible Two-Party System: Political Science, Policy Science, or Pseudo-Science?" *The American Political Science Review* (December 1971).

Sheehan, Colleen. "Madison's Party Press Essays." *Interpretation* (Spring 1990).

Wilson, Woodrow. "The Study of Administration." *Political Science Quarterly* (June 1887).

Index

127

About the Author

Donald V. Weatherman is the John Dyer Trimble Sr. Professor of Political Philosophy at Lyon College. In addition to his interests in political parties and the American founding, he has written articles on civic education and the presidency. He received his B.A. from California State University at Los Angeles and his M.A. and Ph.D. from Claremont Graduate School.